SECRET SUTRAS

PATANJALI'S PATH TO LIBERATION

NIRVANA

ALSO BY NIRVANA

For permission requests, contact
Nirvana Foundation
Email: info@nirvana.foundation
Website: www.nirvana.foundation

ACKNOWLEDGMENT

The whole universe has to come together to move a single blade of grass. This book would not have been possible without the support of everything that has ever happened. I am especially grateful to my students, who record, transcribe, edit, and publish my talks.

TABLE OF CONTENTS

INTRODUCTION

Yoga, originating from the ancient lands of India, represents the pinnacle of spiritual practice and the profound quest for self-knowledge. It offers not just physical or mental health benefits, but a path to ultimate liberation - freedom from the incessant fluctuations of the mind, the temporary allure of sense pleasures, and the inevitable pains of earthly existence.

At the heart of the yogic journey, as noted by the sage Patanjali, are the eight limbs that lead from the do's and don'ts to the sublime state of samadhi. These stages, similar to the Eightfold Path of Buddha, offer a scientific, intuitive blueprint for awakening. The methodology of "The Yoga Sutras of Patanjali" begins with the external - our actions and desires - and goes inward to the core of our being, compelling us to drop all preconceived notions about ourselves and existence.

This discipline is not about arbitrary restrictions but a deep, transformative process that aligns actions, thoughts, and spirit in a harmonious ascent toward self-realization. Unlike the simplistic actions of daily life driven by direct needs like thirst or hunger, the yogic path demands consistency, patience, and unwavering discipline. It insists on a comprehensive engagement with each step, embodying the idea that true transformation is thorough and all-encompassing.

Patanjali does not mince words when describing the physical aspects of yoga - yogasana. Often mistaken for mere physical exercise, true yogasana is an exploration into the deeper currents of yogic discipline, where each posture serves as a gateway to higher awareness, rather than an end in itself.

The culmination of yoga, samadhi, is described not as an end but a profound deepening into the essence of consciousness. Patanjali's teachings suggest that this ultimate state is not merely about self-absorption but about reaching a point where the self extends beyond the individual, merging into a universal presence. This state transcends personal identity and the constructs of the individual mind, achieving a boundless realization of oneness with all existence.

This book, derived from the wisdom of Patanjali and illuminated by the enlightened teacher Nirvana, is not just a guide but a call to action - a prompt to embark on the most significant journey you will ever undertake, the journey within. It invites you to embrace yoga not just as a practice but as a transformational path that promises the greatest of all revelations: the discovery of your true self, the understanding of your purpose, and the liberation from all forms of bondage.

Whether you are an experienced meditator or just beginning, the journey inward is inevitable for those who seek to understand their true nature. This book aims to guide, enlighten, and inspire you to initiate that journey, offering the keys to unlock profound spiritual depths and achieve the ultimate in self-realization.

Secret Sutras

YOGA

Yoga, ancient India's greatest contribution to the world, stands as the science of the soul and the art of self-discovery. It is a path to ultimate liberation, offering freedom from the relentless chatter of thoughts, the fleeting allure of sense pleasures, and the inevitable pain and suffering of life. The word "yoga" originates from the Sanskrit "yuj," meaning to yoke or join, symbolizing the union and balance between mind, body, and spirit.

Yoga is an irreversible transformation, a journey from lower states of consciousness to higher ones, from darkness to light. It is the predecessor of all spiritual practices, encompassing even meditation, which is but one part of its vast scope. To truly grasp the profound essence of yoga, one must recognize that sitting still, closing the eyes, and focusing on the breath - the core of meditation - is merely a single step in the all-encompassing journey of yoga.

MORE THAN GYMNASTICS

Yoga begins externally, starting with the world, your senses, and your experiences. It lays out what you should and should not do, guided by moral principles of right and wrong. It addresses the foundational conditions necessary for deepening meditation. In this sense, yoga is complete; it lacks nothing. If yoga is the source of all spiritual knowledge and great wisdom leading to awakening, then Patanjali is considered the father of yoga - not because he created or invented it, but through his commentary on the yoga sutras. These texts are so ancient that their origins are unknown; we do not even know who wrote them. What we do know is that like a massive mountain whose peak disappears into the clouds, yoga's antiquity extends far beyond our sight, inspiring awe as we acknowledge its ancient origins without knowing its precise source.

Everything we know about yoga is derived from commentaries and discourses given by awakened individuals. Patanjali, for example, is not creating but expanding on the yoga sutras through his discourse, which is regarded as the pinnacle description of yoga. He adheres closely to the source, ensuring his words are devoid of superfluousness or unnecessary details, maintaining a strict focus on the core purpose of yoga. His proximity to yoga is so profound that it almost seems he is discussing something entirely different.

For the Western mind, yoga is often perceived merely as gymnastics. It is seen as a physical practice limited to twisting the body into various shapes, with a focus on the enjoyment derived from the extent to which one can contort their body. This keeps yoga very limited, focusing predominantly on just one of its aspects. In Patanjali's Ashtanga Yoga, which comprises eight limbs, only one limb, called asana or posture, is emphasized. Patanjali himself dedicates merely two verses to asana in his entire yoga sutras, which contain hundreds of verses. However, for many in the West, these postures define the entirety of yoga; the rest - moral principles, deep meditation, and the pursuit of awakening through samadhi - is often disregarded as uninteresting or boring.

In many contemporary yoga schools or studios, there is a lack of holistic understanding that the body is being used as a vehicle to transcend to higher states of consciousness. Instead, yoga is taught primarily as a form of relaxation and unwinding for the body. Naturally, focusing so closely on the body can also relax the mind to some extent. There is nothing inherently wrong with restricting yoga to physical practices; it's not a distortion or a crime. However, this approach is merely a beginning - it does not move forward, expand, or embrace yoga as the ultimate solution for all life's problems or as a transformative way of life. It is seen instead as an exercise to be practiced for perhaps an hour each day.

There is no true understanding of the word "yoga" without understanding what a "yogi" is. A yogi is not merely a meditator, a gymnast, an intellectual philosopher, nor someone filled with knowledge. A yogi is someone so deeply immersed in the process of seeking and searching that they become the embodiment of that search. They see nothing but their pursuit, regardless of where they are or what they experience - they have become the search itself. Western culture recognizes great effort and accomplishment but is unfamiliar with the concept of penance. There is nothing in the Western mindset that is seen as worthy of penance; the closest concept is hard work. For instance, to advance from an ordinary employee to a manager overseeing many people, one does not engage in penance but works toward the goal. Achievements in the world are gained through action because the structures of the world are built on further actions.

Climbing the Spiritual Tree

However, to discover something genuine, something inherently yours, something that completes you, mere effort is insufficient and lacks the necessary conviction. Effort, by its nature, is finite and tied to specific durations and actions. If every moment of life is defined by effort, then the concept of effort loses meaning. It becomes routine: seeing a tree with an apple, you might decide to exert effort to walk to the tree and climb it to get the apple. The world, in this analogy, is like the apple tree, constantly requiring effort.

Spirituality presents a completely different kind of tree. This tree stands before you, making it clear that climbing will not yield any apples. Effort here is futile. While visible, and though you can see the apples, the method to obtain them is entirely unique. You must go inward; you need to become the apple tree, you must transform into the apples themselves. Yet, often the response is to revert to effort, to seek another apple tree - one that can be simply climbed and harvested. The spiritual tree is distinct; it isn't actually there in a physical sense. All the terms we use to describe the inward journey are merely symbolic. Even yoga, which signifies the union of mind, body, and spirit - the ultimate science of awakening - holds no physical relevance in the outer world. You cannot achieve this union to accomplish external objectives because, externally, that union is unnecessary.

In various situations, you might use your mind, your body, or connect with your spirit. In the external world, it's entirely feasible to function while being disconnected; there's no requirement to be unified. However, in the internal world, you can't operate effectively while divided - you must integrate the mind, body, and spirit. How, then, do you climb a tree that doesn't physically exist? If you try to climb it, you'll realize there's nothing tangible to hold onto - the branches are just ideas, and the words are merely theoretical. Trying to physically climb such a tree would only result in falling.

This is where the concept of yoga or penance becomes relevant. You need to approach this climb in a way that it transforms into an internal longing, an inward striving. Yes, there is effort involved in yoga, but this effort is internal and far from ordinary. It is an effort that breaks all conventional limits, transforming into something profoundly new, which we call "penance."

There is a word in Sanskrit called "tapas." A yogi is someone who is engaged in tapas, not only during moments of seated meditation but also when he is fully active - walking and interacting with the world.

He is always mindful of his ultimate destination, constantly seeking that singular truth in everything. This state is what we refer to as being in tapas. The term "tapas" stems from the root word "tapa," which means heat. Thus, when someone is in tapas, they are focusing their awareness, energy, and attention to a singular point, intensely heating it. This heat escalates to a level that eventually melts away all life's impurities. Tapas involves a relentless focus on the core issue - be it the mind or the body. It's about using the heat of your awareness to purify your thoughts and actions, ultimately freeing you from the bondages of life.

"The Yoga Sutras of Patanjali" provides a straightforward, direct, and complete methodology for transformation. This isn't just any transformation; it is the ultimate transformation, the answer to all your questions. There is no other way to approach yoga than with a full commitment to transform yourself entirely. Approaching yoga half-heartedly can lead to misinterpretations, transforming it into mere gymnastics as often seen in the West, or into a pursuit of mysterious powers.

For example, Paramahamsa Yogananda is considered a yogi, and his book, "Autobiography of a Yogi," uses the term 'yogi' but discusses something entirely different. Reading "Autobiography of a Yogi" will not make you a yogi; instead, it may leave you fascinated with miracles, which is a diversion. The book is filled with stories about Yogananda meeting various saints who have acquired different siddhis, or powers, which can sidetrack a reader from the true essence of yoga. The focus on these miraculous powers can prevent one from achieving the deeper, transformational aspects of yoga that Patanjali described.

Patanjali warns that the pursuit of siddhis represents a potential deviation in the practice of yoga. It's a pitfall that practitioners need to be vigilant about. As you deepen your understanding of your mind and body, you might indeed feel that you have acquired powers beyond those of ordinary individuals. You may feel as though you perceive more, can predict future events, or influence others' thoughts and actions. In the realm of the mind, this can give you a sense of enhanced capability because you are more aware of your thoughts than someone who has not embarked on an inward journey. What is hidden to them is visible to you, granting you a certain power in that regard.

However, exercising these powers can be deceptive. The only true power is the ultimate knowledge of who you are. All other powers, or siddhis, that you acquire along the way are temporary and can distract from the true goal of yoga. These abilities - seeing more than others, predicting the future, influencing actions - are superficial compared to the profound self-realization that yoga aims to achieve.

Regarding Paramahamsa Yogananda's "Autobiography of a Yogi," the book emphasizes these siddhis, focusing on the realm of the unconscious and the miraculous. This emphasis can mislead practitioners about the true essence of yoga. Yogananda's interpretation of Kriya Yoga as a method of seeking divine intervention for enlightenment diverges from the traditional meaning. Traditionally, Kriya Yoga involves performing actions (kriya) with detachment and awareness, turning every action into a transformative process (yoga). This approach aligns with the foundational belief that every conscious action can become a path to self-realization.

Patanjali's perspective on yoga is holistic, focusing on meditation and the transmutation of both mind and body, rather than on seeking miracles or external exercises. However, Paramahansa Yogananda's interpretation of Kriya Yoga, as presented in his teachings, differs significantly. He suggests a version of Kriya Yoga where effort and meditation are downplayed in favor of simply asking for divine grace. This interpretation has led many to believe that they need not engage in diligent practice or effort but merely need to request what they desire - be it wealth, fame, or other worldly gains. This understanding can mislead practitioners into thinking that spiritual achievements can be obtained without personal effort, which is contrary to traditional teachings. Such an approach turns Kriya Yoga into something worldly and external, losing the inward focus essential for true yogic practice. These practitioners, though they may believe they are receiving their gains through divine grace, are missing the point of yoga as Patanjali taught it.

In authentic yogic practice, the phase where one believes they have acquired special powers or insights should be viewed as a minor and potentially dangerous stage. It's a point where the ego might find a foothold, tempting one to linger there, impressed with oneself relative to others. This is a seductive ledge where one can get stuck, reveling in the illusion of being special and having something valuable to teach others. This interpretation and application of Kriya Yoga by Yogananda can be misleading, suggesting that enlightenment or significant spiritual progress can be achieved merely through the grace received by asking, without the need for deep meditation and personal transformation. This overlooks the rigorous self-effort and introspection that are fundamental to the true yogic path as outlined by Patanjali.

Just because someone claims to be enlightened does not necessarily make it so. Enlightenment should be discerned through the teachings themselves - whether they can genuinely lead others to enlightenment defines a true enlightened teacher. The label "paramahansa," which was adopted by Yogananda, refers to a very high state of spiritual purity. In Sanskrit, "paramahansa" translates to the "great swan," a symbol traditionally associated with purity and spiritual elevation. The prefix "parama" indicates the highest or ultimate. "hansa" symbolizes purity and is often depicted as a white swan, representing cleanliness and transcendence. Thus, "Paramahansa" signifies the zenith of purity - the greatest of all swans.

Despite Yogananda's use of this esteemed title, the approach he popularized in the West, which focused heavily on miraculous powers (siddhis), deviates from the deeper, more austere path of yoga that Patanjali describes. His teachings, particularly appealing to the Western audience, emphasized the acquisition of powers, resonating with a cultural fascination with dominance and control. This appeal can be traced back to historical philosophies that prioritize power, as seen in Greek and Roman cultures, which have deeply influenced Western thought.

Yogananda's portrayal of yoga, filled with tales of supernatural abilities, catered to this mindset - a mindset that often seeks validation through the demonstration of power or control. This perspective can overshadow the core yogic principle of inner transformation and self-realization, enticing followers instead with the promise of gaining extraordinary abilities. This approach can mislead sincere seekers from the essence of yoga, which is about transcending the ego and achieving a profound inner unity and purity, the true marks of a "Paramahamsa."

Here comes a man who has cleverly understood the psychological framework of the Western mind and presented Eastern yoga, omitting its most important aspects because he himself does not understand them. He has tailored yoga in a way that connects with and appeals to the Western mindset, with utter disregard for truth and the need to genuinely help an individual. The book is designed to deceive the mind, which is why it has been successful and is regarded as one of the greatest books written on yoga. In reality, it is utter rubbish. In fact, the British media have called him the "father of yoga." Anyone familiar with yoga, especially those who have read Patanjali's Yoga Sutras and then compare them to Yogananda's "Autobiography of a Yogi," will see the difference. One represents the pinnacle of human awareness and understanding, while the other is mere trickery. Yoga is neither gymnastics nor a search for mystical powers. You do not become a yogi to gain power; you become a yogi to understand the true nature of life. A yogi is someone who is evolving into a delicate flower, not a cunning magician.

A yogi is not trying to torture his body; rather, he aims to utilize it. The body is a crucial tool for a yogi. He cherishes his body, viewing it as a method or technique through which he can ascend to higher levels of awareness. Thus, yoga is neither about self-mortification nor self-glorification. There are numerous examples of individuals who have misunderstood yoga, transforming it into either a physically arduous process or a mentally stimulating and entertaining activity. However, real yoga is something entirely different. Patanjali introduces us to the true essence of yoga.

Nobody knows if his name was really Patanjali. He is thought to have lived around the second or third century BC. There is also a debate about whether he was one person or a compilation of several individuals who contributed to the commentary. This speculation arises because the work attributed to him is so extraordinary that it seems unlikely to have been the effort of just one individual. However, such skepticism may stem from a modern perspective; ancients were often much more capable. They were not as distracted as people are today. Once they dedicated themselves to a task, they could produce extraordinary works.

For example, consider sage Vyasa's work, the "Mahābhārata." The sheer volume of the book and the depth of insight and understanding of life it offers make one wonder if it is indeed the work of a single individual. Yet, it was written by one man. So was "The Yoga Sutras of Patanjali." Patanjali was an individual, not a collection of individuals. In fact, many ancient scriptures, which actually come from individuals, are attributed to groups because the work is so phenomenal that it is hard to believe it comes from one person. Individuals can produce extraordinary work; groups can only organize things. If there is something unique or original, it can safely be concluded that it comes from the depths of an individual. Patanjali was an individual. Whether his actual name was Patanjali or not is immaterial. The name Patanjali means "a blessing that has descended from the heavens." So, in a way, it's a name that perfectly symbolizes what he represented. His discourse on yoga is so pure and transformative that if you were a student, you would bestow this name upon a teacher and call him "Patanjali." Patanjali is usually symbolically represented as a five-headed serpent descending from heaven. 'pata' also means snake, which is why depictions of Patanjali are always accompanied by a snake. He is a yogi sitting in meditation with a five-headed snake above him. It's a symbolic representation of something meaningful descending from the heavens.

BECOMING A YOGI

As you move toward self-realization and embrace your true nature, you are essentially journeying toward the yogic ocean. The deeper you are yearning for truth and the stronger your longing, the closer you become to being a yogi. A yogi is someone who is in a state of penance at all times. He is mindful, meditative, watchful, and aware at every moment.

Let's get into the methods of the eight limbs of ashtanga yoga. Each one must be explored in depth, as each step leads to the next. Without understanding the first step, you cannot proceed to the second; there's no skipping steps. Patanjali is very precise; he is a man of few words. He conveys the entire sutra in one line. Now, what is a sutra? "Sutra" is a beautiful word itself, deriving from the Sanskrit root "siv," which means to sew. A sutra is essentially the process of joining a few things together to create a garland. A yoga sutra is like stringing together a few words to create a beautiful pearl necklace of a sentence. By its very nature, a sutra cannot be too long. You will not find a sutra that spans half a page, just as you would not find a pearl necklace that is one meter long. A sutra is short, very concise, and every word within it is precious. Not one word can be left out; nothing is unimportant in a sutra. Each word is a precious pearl, a precious gem.

Patanjali is very concise in his description of yoga and he gets straight to the point because he is not trying to convince or boast about his knowledge. He offers the yoga sutras as a prescription. Imagine visiting a doctor: after diagnosing your problem, the doctor will write the solution in one line - this is the medicine, take it this many times a day. That's it. He won't write a lengthy dissertation on the problem because a prescription is sufficient. Patanjali's approach is just as precise. He is a physician, a practitioner of yoga, offering his prescription for the sickness called "you."

When you approach Patanjali, you go to heal yourself. You cannot come with an argumentative mind because you won't find any argument from his side. He'll say, "Either you take it or leave it; it's up to you. This is the method. I'm not trying to convince you." Patanjali assumes you should already be convinced before coming to him. If you still believe you can find what you're looking for in the outside world, then continue your search outside. This means you have not yet realized the futility of searching externally.

You are still enchanted by life and believe that the answers lie outside. In this case, Patanjali assumes you are not ready for yoga. He speaks only to those who are ready.

Now, what makes you ready for yoga? You are ready to die. This means you are ready to forget everything you were, to be reborn, and to view your life anew. You approach yoga as a child who knows nothing, while the teacher is a wise sage, your grandfather in wisdom, understanding, and life experience. You are a baby sitting in front of him, asking for the method. You are not his equal, nor is he your friend. You are not there to argue about what works and what doesn't. You are in a mode of receiving, with wide-open eyes and ears, fresh and new. That is the starting point of yoga.

Let's begin with Patanjali's words:

When you are inspired by some great purpose, some extraordinary project, all your thoughts break their bonds. Your mind transcends limitations, your consciousness expands in every direction, and you find yourself in a new, great, and wonderful world. Dormant forces, faculties, and talents become alive, and you discover yourself to be a far greater person by far than you ever dreamed yourself to be.

He is opening your mind to the greatest possibilities of yoga. He is saying that there will come a moment in your life when you are ready to receive something extraordinary - a wisdom, a knowledge, an understanding that can end your misery and confusion. In the presence of such knowledge, your limitations will break, and you will begin to see that you are ready for something grand and momentous. Nothing can supersede yoga in this regard.

If you were to seek one knowledge, one skill, one method, and be willing to remain ignorant of everything else in life, you should seek yoga. It is the ultimate science, the science of union that brings together your mind, body, and spirit. Only this much is required. Nothing is missing in you, but you are divided. Your mind is in one part of the world, your body in another, and your spirit somewhere in outer space. Nothing is missing, but the distance you have put between them fills your life with effort. Every moment of living is an effort because you have to run from the mind to the body to the spirit.

Yoga brings the mind, body, and spirit together. That is all that is required. When your mind is where your body is, and your spirit is aligned with both, you become whole. When all three are available to you, you can think when you want to think, feel when you want to feel, move when you want to move, and drop everything to become free when desired. Control over these faculties is possible only when they are close by, within your reach. If you have to chase after them or make appointments to meet them, then you are not in control - they are.

The mind demands you come to it, knock on its door, ask for permission, and then it decides whether to respond. Yoga addresses this problem of disconnection. It identifies disconnection as the root issue. The only prerequisite for diving into the mysterious, magnificent world of yoga is courage. You can approach yoga in many different ways, but you cannot be a yogi without courage. A coward can never be a yogi because the journey involves moving toward the unknown and being ready to let go of your past. It takes great courage to say, "I want to relive my life. I want to see it differently."

Karen Armstrong, when talking about Buddha, says that when Buddha left his palace and went into the forest in search of truth, he did not go singing and dancing. He did not go joyfully. His heart was trembling with fear. Buddha himself later recollected that he felt like he died every time he heard any noise in the forest, such as the rustling of leaves or the footsteps of a deer. His hair would stand on end. It wasn't just fear; it was terror because he was in a completely unknown and vulnerable environment.

We often overlook these details. We focus on the end result: he left the palace, went into the forest, and became enlightened. It sounds great, but consider the immense courage it took to go through that process. He was a yogi, and it is this courage that defines a yogi. The starting point of diving into yoga and understanding Patanjali is to drop your timid, fearful self and be open to accepting something new - to be courageous enough to walk the path. His words are steps, they are ladders, meant to be used to descend into the depths of your being. And those depths are great - your inner self is not shallow; it is very deep. With courage as the starting point, we can descend into the magical realm of yoga.

Yamas - The Don'ts

Patanjali outlines eight steps to awakening, starting from the outermost layer of experiences and leading all the way to samadhi. I don't think it's coincidental that Buddha also outlines eight steps, known as the Eightfold Path - right action, right speech, right thought, and so on. However, Patanjali's differentiation is more scientific, more intuitive, and more encompassing. It stays true to the essence of yoga. It is crucial to understand that the moment you decide to inquire into the nature of reality through yogic practices, all arbitrary separations between who you think you are and what you think existence is should be dropped.

Yoga is not just about transforming the body or the mind, nor is it merely about understanding your life. Yoga is about understanding life itself in its entirety. In yoga, nothing can remain unknown. If anything remains hidden from you, then your search has not ended. Your search concludes when everything becomes known. This may seem like a lofty quest, almost impossible, but that is the essence of yoga. It is a practice that moves you from illusion to what you think is impossible, from being a limited expression of life to becoming the source itself.

Yoga is concerned with totality. It is not focused on solving your individual problems. It identifies one fundamental issue: that you are something to be experienced, something to be lived, something to be absorbed in. Currently, you are searching for experiences, shifting from a phenomenon of being to a phenomenon of becoming. You are constantly trying to become something. You become movement, change, a continuous search, which, by the very definition of change and movement, keeps you in a state of eternal unrest and prevents you from settling down.

If you cannot simply "be," then there is no meaning in "becoming," because even in becoming, you must first be. Being is your primary state; everything else happens around that state of being. Because you have forgotten this fundamental state of being, yoga sees this as the only problem to be solved. You are not separate from the ultimate reality. Once you fully know yourself, you will know everything there is to know.

While the quest of yoga is very lofty, encompassing the whole universe, it is also very simple and straightforward. It does not allow for any deviation. Yoga identifies the problem and addresses only that problem. Patanjali starts from the outermost, which he calls yamas, or the things you should not do. Even before understanding what you need to do to become a yogi, what you need to learn, understand, and practice, you must start from where you are. The most important thing to understand initially is what not to do - the non-doing that will put you in a natural space of yoga. Because you are already doing so much, doing has become your life. While yoga, in words, is about doing something, its essence is the art of non-doing. The ultimate purpose of yoga is to be in union, to be in the totality of experiences, to be at the center of the totality of life.

What is stopping you from simply being? It is all that you're doing. So, identifying where you are lost, what activities you are lost in, becomes the first and most important step. Almost all religions cover this aspect, but the only difference is that they stop there. What yoga refers to as Yamas, or moral principles - such as speaking the truth, not stealing, not killing, and watching your sense pleasures - are outlined by Patanjali as the starting point for a deeper inquiry within yourself. For religions, however, this is both the starting and the ending point. They know nothing beyond this initial phase. That is why most religions are only concerned with the outermost layer of spirituality, the first limb of yoga, which involves cultivating a set of moral guidelines that help you avoid certain actions.

This is the only step where decisions must be made consciously to not do certain things, to control your mind, actions, and activities. This necessity arises because you are not yet connected with that space from where you can act intuitively, with your true center from which every action is complementary in nature and illuminates your being. Since you are lost in the mind, you cannot access this space without restrictions, rules, or certain guidelines and principles. But remember, this is only the starting point.

In a way, the outermost layer is the first step, where you are given certain commandments and rules. Every teacher, whether a Buddhist monk or a Hindu yogi, starts by introducing you to your own world of activities. Let's say, for example, you are an incessant liar. While this may seem unrelated to whether you can become enlightened or go deep into your being, it is nonetheless addressed. The teacher tells you to stop lying - not because he is concerned with the external effects of your actions on others, but because he is concerned with you.

Why does he instruct you to stop lying? If you're lying on the outside, and you've become proficient at it or see value in it, it's likely that you are also lying to yourself internally. How can you embark on the greatest journey of your life - a journey filled with obstacles and uncertainties, a journey through the unknown territories of your mind and body to reach your ultimate self - if you cannot be honest with yourself? The teacher sees that your lying is an obstacle. He's not really concerned about the act of lying per se, but rather whether you are capable of having an honest conversation with yourself. When you experience something internally, can you recognize it for what it is? Can you avoid exaggerating or over-glorifying it? When you understand the ramifications of lying and how easily it can obscure the truth, it becomes clear why honesty is an essential, almost foundational step in turning inward.

You cannot find honesty on the inside, because it is an action, something you have been doing. In the inner world, there is neither lying nor speaking the truth. There will come a point when conversations are no longer necessary. Once you have reached a zone of stillness and silence, your moral principles and how you have engaged with the world cease to matter. But until you reach that point, you must listen to the conversations in your mind. There is no real distinction between the conversations happening in the outer world and those inside; they are the same. You cannot be truthful on the inside while lying on the outside, because what you are on the inside is what you manifest externally. Thus, the first guidelines are always about the "don'ts" - what not to do. And then the actual journey begins.

There are eight steps for self-transformation, for awakening, each requiring equal amounts of time. While Patanjali spends about ten percent of his energy talking about moral principles, religions dedicate one hundred percent of their energies to this one step, because they know nothing else. The preachers have not turned inward; they see that it is enough to control people with the "don'ts." It provides great satisfaction for them to dictate what you should not do - it's an ego trip. "Don't steal, don't kill, don't covet your neighbor's wife." All these commandments are fascinating, but what do you do with all that? Why am I restricting myself, and what is the purpose?

What does a religion promise? It promises that if you restrict yourself in certain ways, you will go to heaven. Conversely, if you live immorally, without care and concern for yourself and those around you, you will go to hell. That's the judgment. Where have religions faltered? They falter right at the first step by treating these moral guidelines as the ultimate goal. At the end of that step, where the journey inward should begin - towards that heavenly space within - they instead place heaven externally. This blocks off the entire search. This is why you don't become enlightened by reading the Bible. You will not develop a desire to become a yogi by reading the Quran. You won't thirst for awakening when reading the Gita. While the words, the ideas, might seem intuitive and meditative, and not very different from what a teacher truly desiring your awakening might say, there is a lack of understanding. Morality has become an end in itself, rather than just the first step.

Patanjali discusses morality and outlines "don'ts," but these should not be confused with the religious do's and don'ts. The religious prescriptions are often blinding and lacking explanations because they are directed toward an imaginary heaven and hell. That's why if you ask, "Why should I not steal?" you won't get a satisfactory answer. The response is usually a repetition of what has been taught: "It is a commandment, what God instructed, and it is not to be questioned." This type of thinking is futile for yoga.

Yoga demands inquiry. Everything you are told to do or not to do must be questioned. You need to understand these directives to the extent that you begin to follow them intuitively, regardless of external expectations. You won't be concerned about whether these moral principles are strictly imposed from outside because, intuitively, you understand how they benefit you. Moral guidelines are useless unless they are personally meaningful and beneficial.

SATYA - TRUTHFULNESS

The first yama that Patanjali discusses is satya, or truthfulness. He states, "When one is firmly established in truthfulness, the fruits of actions become subservient to him." Consider the profound beauty of this statement. For the person who is rooted in truth, the outcomes of actions become subservient. This means you are not chasing after results; you are engaged in the process because you are truthful to your practice and what you are seeking. There is no need for false justifications. It is only a mind accustomed to lying that tries to cling to every result and make it seem more important than it is.

Truth waits. Truth has infinite patience. It has no need to claim a result when it isn't there. As you start to understand yourself, you will discover precious nuggets of wisdom and unravel hidden parts of yourself. When you're truthful, the specifics of what you uncover become less important. What matters is that you have only begun your journey. Already, you're beginning to see and experience things differently.

This is a clear indication that you're on the right path and should continue.

A truthful mind sets aside the results and stays focused on the path. It's similar to traveling with a plan: you know where you want to go, how long you want to spend there, and what your ultimate destination is. Once you start walking, you will undoubtedly encounter exciting and new things. However, if you are truthful to your journey and acknowledge that your destination is still far away, you will simply notice what's happening around you and keep moving forward.

When you have not separated yourself from your lies, when you don't care about being truthful to yourself, it becomes easy to shift the destination closer. You might think, "There's no need to go that far." You can create your own justifications. For example, you might say, "Look at this tree and the fruits on it. I have never seen anything like it elsewhere. It is the most beautiful tree I've ever seen. What's the necessity to continue this journey further, to spend more time, more energy? I don't think I'll ever find a tree as beautiful as this. Let me sit under this tree for the next twenty days, and then return home." This is why truthfulness is so important.

The conversations that you have within yourself determine your journey and the quality of your internal experiences. If you are not honest about what you are telling yourself, then even before you begin, you would have already deviated from the path. You will find reasons to contradict yourself and your teacher, and very soon, you could be stuck in a world of your own creation, which is precisely where you are now.

Truth, according to Patanjali, is not just about speaking truthfully - it is not merely about words. Patanjali would not be so superficial. If he has spoken about something, there must be a deeper meaning. More importantly, truth is about right intention, not just the words; it is your intention that distinguishes true from false. This is why, in the Bhagavad Gita, Krishna seems to dismiss the basic moral principles that form the foundation of spirituality by saying you can kill, lie, or steal. Meanwhile, Buddha advocates for ahimsa, or non-violence, as the path to salvation, stating that ultimate reality cannot be reached through violence. Yet, Krishna urges Arjuna to fight, creating a paradox.

This leaves many wondering how to reconcile with these teachings. In the outer world, it seems impossible to adhere strictly to these guidelines. Many admit they cannot go a single day without lying; lying is part of humor, a way of navigating life. It's only when people decide to speak the truth that they realize how ingrained lying is in the fabric of daily living. The same goes for non-violence. If you are a meat-eater, how can you reconcile this with a belief system that claims non-violence as the path to salvation? Even if you are a vegetarian, simply walking can result in harm to delicate creatures under your feet. These contradictions highlight the complexity of applying spiritual principles in daily life and suggest that the essence of these teachings - whether from Krishna or Buddha - focuses on the intentions behind our actions rather than the literal interpretation of rules.

This is where intention becomes crucial. Moral guidelines cannot be seen as black-and-white rules. Your intentions must be clear, pure, and true, as they ultimately determine your actions and words. For example, a lie can be justifiable if it aligns with your true intention of self-discovery. This perspective provides morality with its proper framework.

When the central objective is to illuminate the life within you, your moral principles will neither harm you nor others. Without the ultimate purpose of finding your true self, morality becomes nothing more than a whip used to inflict pain on yourself and others. The world is in its current state largely because of this moral pitfall. People are often given rules and commandments without explanations of why they should or should not do something. When they fail to follow these commandments, they are punished. This approach fails to foster genuine understanding or internalization of moral values, leading instead to resentment and compliance out of fear rather than conviction.

We have created a world steeped in non-understanding, lacking explanations, filled with rules, regulations, and punishments. How can an individual truly find themselves in such an environment? It is no coincidence that individuals rarely find themselves in the external world, a world built on the presumption that there is no inner insight. What you seek, according to many religious perspectives, is not within you but somewhere external. This assumption leads to a reliance on commandments rather than guidelines, on rules rather than teachings.

This approach disconnects individuals from their inner selves, directing their search outward instead of encouraging an inward journey. Without the opportunity to explore and understand their own depths, people are often left following external dictates without truly grasping their purpose or aligning them with their personal truths. This disconnect is why many struggle to find genuine fulfillment and understanding in their lives.

The seeker of truth inquires into everything. He will not assume anything. If you tell him to speak the truth, he'll ask why. There is no necessity to speak the truth if it is not necessary. Who is telling you to speak the truth? Remember, just as in meditation, just as in the search for enlightenment, and in yoga, in the process of grand unification, the first step is to recognize that you are your own teacher. You are the arbitrator of what happens inside you. You decide what is right, what is wrong, what is good, and what is bad, because it is your journey. The arbitrary separation between you and the world has been dropped. Now, you're trying to understand everything. If you are trying to understand everything, there cannot be anything left unexplained. If someone tells you that you have to speak the truth because God tells you to, you must reject it right there. You cannot leave anything unknown and move into yoga.

Here, to cover up one unknown - truth - you've invented another unknown called God, introducing two unknowns into the equation. That's too much uncertainty for yoga, which is a scientific exploration, not a debate or philosophical concept, and certainly not just a moral framework. Yoga involves actual physical and mental transformation; it is not superficial. You need to dig deep. So, you must ask, "Why should I speak the truth?" Patanjali himself provides the answer: "When one is firmly established in truthfulness, the fruits of actions become subservient to him." This principle is crucial. On a long journey, not clinging to the fruits of your actions is what allows you to continue.

What has stopped free people from going all the way? What has blocked an individual's journey? It is the assumption that they have already found what they were looking for, thinking, "This is enough. This is what I was searching for." That is why truth is important. You will see that truthfulness is helpful on your journey. It doesn't matter whether it is imposed from outside, or whether everyone around you is truthful, because now it's not just a moral principle - it's a scientific fact that truthfulness aids your progress. The debate ends there, and you move on to the next step.

A joke comes to mind that can help us distinguish between being truthful on the inside and on the outside. The conflict in the world is that if you're truthful all the time, if you just speak the truth openly, you might get into trouble. That's why people often choose not to. There is a way to be truthful on the inside while still telling lies on the outside. Truth and lies are not so much about what you say, but why you say it - the intention behind it.

A man is at a job interview for a position as a janitor. During the interview, the hiring manager asks him, "What is your biggest weakness?" The man thinks for a moment and says, "Honesty." The hiring manager is surprised and asks, "Why is honesty a weakness?" The man replies, "I don't know, but I don't really care what you think." The hiring manager is taken aback and asks, "What do you mean?" The man says, "Well, I'm not really interested in this job. I just came for the free coffee." The hiring manager is annoyed and decides to end the interview. As the man is leaving, he turns to the hiring manager and says, "By the way, your fly is open."

There is no necessity to always be truthful in words. Imposing the arbitrary restriction that every word you speak must be truthful can often lead to trouble. Words are just that - words. Especially within human communities, words are used artfully. What truly determines the quality of those words is the intention behind them. If your intention is to help, to be kind, or to secure a job, then lying is not inherently problematic. In fact, it's nearly impossible to speak a sentence without some form of untruth because language, by its very nature, presents a one-sided argument. You can assert anything and equally present a counterargument. Even your so-called truths can be counter-argued and proven false because language is contextual and immediate. When you analyze what you have said after a while, you might find lies in the same words you once regarded as absolutely true.

This becomes a problem for someone trapped in a strict moral framework, someone not engaged in a yogic exploration of life but stuck in rigid ideas of right and wrong. Such a person is continually filled with guilt. Even if he speaks the truth, he may doubt whether it's the truth or not. Even if he acts in a certain way, because he hasn't understood the consequences of his actions, he is merely following moral guidelines without knowing their outcomes.

For example, consider the moral guideline that charity is good, and that you should help someone who asks for assistance. This seems straightforward and uncomplicated. Imagine a homeless person comes to your doorstep, knocks on your door, and asks for money. He says, "I don't have any food. I'm hungry. I need some money. I saw the cross hanging there, you know, I thought you are a good Christian, and you would give me some money." Now, he's introduced guilt into your decision. If you consider yourself a good Christian, you might feel compelled to give him something.

So, you give him some money. He then buys alcohol, gets drunk, meets with an accident, and dies. If you had not given him the money, he might have lived at least another day. It's a direct consequence; your money inadvertently changed the direction of his life. If you had not given him money, he might have gone to the next door, possibly triggering a different sequence of events where he might have met someone who could have offered him a different perspective on life, pulling him away from his detrimental path.

This scenario is speculative, but it illustrates that your action, meant as a charitable gesture, contributed to his death. This example highlights the complexity of moral decisions and the unintended consequences that can arise, showing that even well-intentioned actions can have unforeseen outcomes.

How would you reconcile with that fact? You acted according to your moral framework, and yet that very framework led to someone's death. How can you not feel guilty? It's a straightforward example. Many actions of a moralist eventually circle back to create more guilt. This is because morality without understanding equates to guilt. Therefore, morality cannot merely be preached; it must be practiced. When you preach morality, you're essentially preaching guilt. Telling someone "do this, don't do that" actually introduces guilt into their mind. It's no surprise that a religious mind often harbors guilt. It lives in pain and misery because it adheres to a moral framework devoid of understanding. Understanding arises from connecting the guidelines to your ultimate destination: Is this action helpful on my journey?

Because you are not on a journey, your search has been obscured. You don't know what to do with these moral principles. Moral principles are essentially guidelines, signposts - take a left, take a right, go straight. The underlying assumption is that you are going somewhere. Only in yoga, only in meditation, are you truly going somewhere. But in the world, where are you going? You're not moving toward a deeper understanding of yourself. There is no clear direction, no defined path. That's why these so-called signposts are confusing. One sign points right, another left, but what do these directions mean? There's no explanation because there's no clear understanding that you are on a journey. Life is a journey to understand everything; it is not merely a process of accumulating experiences. These experiences have meaning. Everything you encounter in life either pushes you closer or takes you farther away from yourself.

ASTEYA - NON-STEALING

The easiest way to understand life is to understand both the journey and the destination. Then, following moral guidelines becomes straightforward. Consider the second sutra, "Asteya," or non-stealing. Patanjali states, "When one is firmly established in non-stealing, all wealth comes to him." Why does Patanjali focus on non-stealing? It's not just about the act of not stealing; it relates to greed. Why do you steal? Because you're greedy. If you're starving and need food, go steal food; moral principles only apply if you're alive. Without life, moral principles are useless.

However, for most people, stealing isn't about survival; it's about the desire to possess more, driven by greed and fear. The more fearful and greedy you are, the more you feel you need. That's why Patanjali emphasizes that when one is firmly established in non-stealing, truly understanding and relinquishing greed, wealth naturally comes to him. Accumulating wealth is acceptable if you understand what true wealth is. Wealth is not merely currency, not just superficial accolades, nor is it about glorifying the ego. Wealth isn't something that satisfies your ego; true wealth is something that exists within you.

Your ability to speak the truth, your capacity to be loving and kind, and your aliveness and awareness -

this is wealth. True wealth is something you are born with; it is not something added to you. True wealth lies in recognizing your inherent abilities: your intelligence, your decision-making skills, your ability to handle life's challenges, your moral strength, your emotional strength, and your psychological strength. This is your true wealth.

What is the point of having all the material wealth if you lack the inner supporting structures? Then you're not truly wealthy. It is said that your wealth is not determined by what you have, but by what you can afford to lose. How much you are willing to lose determines how wealthy you are. Are you wealthy enough to lose? If you cannot lose and still feel wealthy, then what is the use of all your wealth? You are not truly wealthy; you are only attached to an idea of wealth.

True wealth is the ability to say, "I am wealthy on the inside. What I have on the outside is fine, but it does not determine who I am." You don't have to accept this as a moral guideline just because Patanjali says it or because it comes from the yogic tradition. Try to understand it. What happens when you are greedy? It takes you away from your true search. When the actual wealth is inside, your quest for wealth on the outside takes you away from yourself. This is the moral framework behind why you should not steal or be greedy. Stealing creates a sense of guilt, and guilt distances you from your true self. More importantly, when the wealth you seek is inside, the purpose of yoga is to realize this hidden inner wealth. What is the point of stealing external things?

BRAHMACHARYA - CHASTITY

Brahmacharya, which means "chastity" or "moderation," is another principle. Patanjali states that when one is firmly established in chastity or moderation, great vigor is acquired. However, it is often interpreted that Patanjali advocates for celibacy - no sex, no sensual pleasures. If you take this as a moral principle and apply it blindly, you can be sure that you will end up so miserable that your reaction to sex could become excessively intense. This is because sex is a fundamental force, a fundamental energy driving life. You cannot simply impose a moral framework and say, "From now on, I'm not going to have sex. I'm not going to have thoughts of sex." Your whole mind and body are filled with ideas about sex. So, what are you going to do with it?

How does religion deal with it? By condemning sex and everything associated with it - the body originates from sex, the mind originates from sex, your desires originate from sex, and you yourself come from sex.

Consequently, everything connected to it is often condemned.

It is not surprising that religions condemn everything - they condemn the body, the mind, and desires. Why? Because they do not understand. They do not grasp that celibacy is not merely a rule, but an understanding of why. Patanjali is very deliberate when he says, "When one is firmly established in chastity or moderation, great vigor is acquired." He is essentially talking about energy conservation.

He is not advocating celibacy as a rebellion against sex. He has nothing against sex. How could Patanjali be against sex, when sex is one of the pathways through which you can awaken? The use of the body in sexual techniques and the Greek word "orgy," which literally means a communion with the divine, illustrate this point. Patanjali is not opposed to sex. What he is emphasizing is that a great amount of energy is expended in sexual activities, requiring both physical and mental energy. If you are able to moderate - not eliminate - and understand and control this aspect of your life, you will conserve the necessary energy and vigor to explore deeper into yoga.

Yoga requires a great deal of energy. You cannot afford to waste your energy because its source is finite, and you are limited by the capacities of your mind and body. Your body can become exhausted. For example, if you eat too much and then sit in meditation, you'll likely fall asleep due to an energy imbalance. Similarly, if you starve yourself and sit in meditation, you will also fall asleep because of an energy imbalance. That is why, if you try to meditate immediately after sex, you will likely fall asleep; you're too tired from exhausting both your body and your mind. You are not in the optimal state to pursue deep meditation.

In this context, Patanjali advises you to be mindful of sex and to be aware of how energy is being used. He is not condemning sex; he is highlighting that it is an area where much of your energy might be drained. Sex involves more than physical activity; it influences how you arrange your life. Human societies are often structured around the premise that the more successful, wealthy, or famous you are, the more sexual opportunities you may have. This, Patanjali suggests, is a waste of energy. As a yogi, you need to understand this dynamic and the process of desiring.

Again, you don't have to believe this simply because Patanjali says so. Experiment for yourself. Observe how sex affects your meditation. See how much of your energy is occupied by sexual thoughts or activities, and then you will understand where your energy is going and how to better conserve it for your yogic practices.

APARIGRAHA - NON-GREED

The last one is aparigraha, which means non-possessiveness or non-greed. When one is firmly established in non-possessiveness, they gain knowledge of the why and how of existence. Patanjali is introducing you to the concept of detached attachment. It is impossible not to be attached to things, but with a sense of inner detachment, you can find the freedom to explore more about yourself.

Attachment is not beneficial on the path of yoga because it makes you clingy, dependent, and subservient to something outside of yourself. We don't cling to things on the inside; we don't possess things that are internal. Whatever is inside - my thoughts, my dreams, my desires - is inherently mine. The whole idea of possessiveness and clinging applies to the external. If you are clinging to external things, then your energies are being wasted there. You have to put additional effort into detaching yourself from what you are clinging to and turn inward. By cultivating a sense of detachment, you naturally create the right conditions for self-inquiry. These are the only non-doings Patanjali talks about.

That's it. This is the moral framework - simple, intuitive, and easy to understand. There are no gods, no heaven or hell, and no one to punish you in hell for not following these commandments. These are useful guidelines. A student arrives with the intention to learn more about himself, and a yogi advises, "Watch these aspects; they will assist you on your journey." These are merely a few useful tools. Don't cling to these tools or regard them as absolutes etched in stone. Understand them, and don't feel guilty when you're unable to follow them perfectly. As you come to understand why these guidelines are important, you will learn how to use them effectively. Yamas are basic moral guidelines that a seeker uses to keep himself in check; they are not rigid rules but useful guidelines.

Secret Sutras

NIYAMAS - THE DO'S

So, if yamas are the "don'ts," then niyamas are the "do's." After clarifying the don'ts, Patanjali discusses the habits and practices that you can cultivate, which will form the basic framework for the rest of your yogic journey. A strong foundation is essential. The word 'niyama' itself means 'rule.' The restrictions that you place on yourself to cultivate certain behaviors are collectively referred to as niyamas or rules. You cannot begin your yogic journey without certain rules. However, these rules are not restrictions in the truest sense; they are essentially guidelines. You can progress on the path without these rules, but somewhere along the journey, you will need to come back and revisit them.

There is a great temptation to skip certain steps in yoga. The moment you become aware of something deeper, something you can experience, you will rush to experience it. This is the nature of the mind, which always moves toward greater reward and satisfaction. Herein lies its biggest problem: In the world, you're seeking only momentary pleasures - pleasures that don't last for more than a few minutes - and pursuing them vigorously. Sometimes, skipping all the steps makes sense. If you're thirsty, you simply drink water. If you're hungry, you eat. If you feel like resting, you rest. If you feel like moving, you move. In the outside world, actions and their consequences are restrictive and easily observable. "If I do this, I get this; if I don't do this, I might not get this." The pleasure-seeking mechanism is momentary. Therefore, you really don't follow any steps in the outer world. What you recognize as discipline is merely arrangement and organization by time, place, and events - that's about it.

Yogic discipline is something entirely different. In yoga, discipline is not an additional requirement; it is the path itself. Discipline is the method. In the outer world, you can skip steps, but in the inner world, if you skip steps, sooner or later, you will have to return and complete the step you missed.

Let's go back to our basic understanding of yoga. What is it? It is total transformation. Nothing can be left out. Therefore, you cannot set the time and duration of this transformation. If you are seeking a limited transformation, you might set a restriction and say, "This is what I want, and I want to experience it by this time. Whatever I can experience within, let's say, the next three months, I will accept, but I cannot devote any more time to this activity." You cannot do that with yoga. Because the very nature of transformation in yoga is total and complete, you cannot skip steps.

The first step is to identify external things you can avoid. This will help you stay rooted and focused on the task. Then come the "do's," which will build the foundation. Literally, niyama is the stage where you dig the foundation, pour the concrete, and ensure that you're doing it in such a way that your structure can stand firm. You don't do it half-heartedly, and worst of all, you don't leave it incomplete. What is the point of building a house on an incomplete foundation? While you might feel that you are progressing quickly and understanding more, if the foundation is not right, eventually, you will find your practice wobbly.

What is this foundation? Patanjali provides beautiful verses that not only offer a sturdy platform to begin the journey but also something that we can carry forward throughout our journey. Niyamas can be used as constant companions on the yogic path. You can keep referring back to them, readjusting your journey. In this way, these rules provide a framework for tuning your practice. To put it another way, Patanjali's niyamas are akin to Buddha's middle path. These niyamas will help you stay the course and avoid extremes. It is not surprising that there is a great parallel between Patanjali's words and Buddha's words. It is only in words that they appear to be talking about something different, but they are referring to the same destination. While Buddha's emphasis was on mindfulness and meditation, Patanjali also leads to mindfulness and meditation, but he starts with the prerequisites. Even before coming to meditation, you need to understand certain rules, certain guidelines.

SAUCHA - PURITY

The first one, "saucha" or "purity," involves cleanliness and purity of both body and mind, which fosters a disposition for self-study and a sense of contentment. Patanjali isn't just talking about the physical aspect of keeping your body clean, although that is a requirement. He places significant emphasis on the purity of the mind. What does he mean by purity of the mind? Isn't that what you're ultimately trying to attain? Your mind is filled with all kinds of thoughts; you're stressed, anxious, and worried, and you aim to use the yogic path to purify your mind to eventually experience clarity. Here, Patanjali suggests that you need to cultivate purity before you embark on the journey. Purity is an initial step. He is indicating that there are actions you can take consciously with your mind that make it a fertile ground for your practice. Yes, yoga purifies your mind and your body, but this purification is not just at the surface level. Surface-level purification can be achieved consciously, because you can observe your thoughts and actions. Anything you can observe, you can influence and change.

The reason you embark on a yogic journey is that so much about you remains unknown. You are just the tip of the iceberg; what you know about yourself is merely the surface. The bulk of the iceberg is hidden. If you are able to recognize problems in your life, these are only small parts of a larger issue. All the emotions you can identify - fear, pain, anger, worry - while they seem to appear and disappear randomly, are actually supported by a larger structure beneath them. This is what yoga addresses. This deeper purification targets the underlying causes. At the surface level, you can recognize and change simpler things.

One thing within your control is assessing how far you have strayed from your simple, childlike nature. You know what it is to be like a child: that innate sense of wonder, the eagerness to learn and explore. You also recognize those moments when these innate qualities - those childlike traits - are overshadowed by responsibilities, social expectations, and religious structures, all of which you have imposed upon yourself. Therefore, even before you go into your inner world you need to make some adjustments in the realm of your mind.

Yes, you need to keep your body clean. This is not hard to understand. It is difficult to feel close to your body when it is not clean. In yoga, you will spend a lot of time with your body; after all, yoga is fundamentally about the body. Only in the final stage, samadhi, will you transcend the body. Until then, it is always with you. Throughout all the steps, keeping it clean is not a bad idea.

The reason Patanjali emphasizes cleanliness is due to a prevalent misunderstanding at the time. There was a belief that a yogi or an ascetic need not maintain personal hygiene. Patanjali was aware of such practices. Taking care of oneself and keeping clean was often seen as a waste of time because the body was so condemned that no importance was placed on its care. For many, self-mortification was seen as the path. They viewed their bodies as obstacles and even developed a sense of loathing towards them. Thus, they neglected to keep their bodies clean, healthy, and comfortable.

This was not just during Patanjali's time. Even now, many yogis don't prioritize cleanliness. For example, if you were to visit yogis in India who have left home, who have abandoned everything familiar, and who are living in the foothills of the Himalayas, you might find it challenging to approach them. Some of them are so unkempt that you cannot even get close enough for a conversation. They don't wash their hair, which over months or even years accumulates dirt, grime, and oiliness, resulting in what is recognized as matted hair. For a yogi, this is not a style choice; it's a result of neglect. Their hair becomes so matted that it is impossible to comb or manage.

Furthermore, look at their nails. They are unkept, and some yogis even flaunt their long nails, growing them throughout their lives. They see these practices as achievements, as they provide ego satisfaction from doing something different from everyone else. While others spend time cutting their nails, washing their hair, and keeping their bodies clean, these yogis view such practices as wasteful. However, this attitude does not reflect the true yogi but rather a delusional yogi who has forgotten the actual principles of yoga.

There are more people who have misunderstood yoga than those who have truly grasped it. Many call themselves yogis but know nothing about yoga. They think a yogi is an ascetic who lives like a wild animal, comparing themselves to animals. This comparison exists within yoga. They have strayed so far from their true nature and become so structured in their thinking, so mechanical, that to become a yogi, you must first reconnect with your animal nature and then progress toward your divine nature. Your animal nature serves as an intermediary. Yogis have emphasized the need to connect with their animal nature, which really means reconnecting with your primal instincts - being simple in the moment, not worrying too much about tomorrow, and not spending all your time and effort accumulating things. Returning to your animal nature actually means recognizing the simple, primal being that you are. When this is misunderstood, some take it literally and decide to live like animals, questioning why they should wash their hair or bodies since no animal does. However, they fail to understand that animals keep themselves clean through their own mechanisms and methods, which you do not know.

You were born as a human being and raised within a social structure, so your understanding of cleanliness differs from theirs. As a result, you can't even get close to these so-called yogis. They stink, and they call this their practice, their sadhana. Almost every mystical culture has produced such individuals. In Hindu culture, this is openly visible. You see yogis who look as though they could die at any moment. They eat once a day, sleep on the floor, don't bathe, and live in crematoriums. They smear their bodies with ashes because Shiva did that. However, they don't realize that it's a symbolic representation. Shiva conquered death - he did not fear it, which is symbolized by the garland of skulls he wears. Yet, there are these so-called yogis who eat out of human skulls and smear their bodies with the ashes of human remains.

Even in Christian mysticism, there are mystics who took this self-mortification, this disdain for the body, to extreme levels. Suso, a Christian mystic, slept on a bed of nails, believing it brought him closer to Jesus. There are mystics who have cleaned the wounds of people with their tongues, removing pus and blood, because they believed it would bring them closer to Jesus. Such behaviors are often encouraged and glorified. It is said that a mystic who completely lets go of any attachment to the body, who does not differentiate between food and excrement, will go straight to Jesus. I'm not making this up. Every mystical tradition is filled with examples of people who have grossly misunderstood the simple idea of using the body to transcend to a higher realm. Once you start hating the body, you get stuck.

Patanjali emphasizes the importance of purifying both the body and the mind. He is clear about the necessity of keeping the body clean; once you recognize this need, all other aspects of body care come into play. You must keep it healthy and ensure it has enough energy. There's no need to overanalyze what he means by purity of the body - you know what it means for the body to be pure. Yoga is not about self-mortification; it's about loving your body. Your body is your vehicle; if it isn't functioning properly, you cannot progress very far. It can take you from this realm to a higher one and be your constant companion. Thus, there's no other option but to keep it clean.

Then he addresses the mind. Primarily, there are two obstacles: one is the conditioning you received from your upbringing, and the other is your religious conditioning. These two forces have shaped most of the structures of the mind. It is often said that every person is trying to either live up to their father's expectations or make up for their father's mistakes. In many ways, this holds true. Each individual is often striving to meet someone else's expectations, and more often than not, these are the expectations of their parents. Because they set the rules and the guidelines and they see you as an extension of themselves, whether they intend to or not, they fill your mind with ideas. These ideas have nothing to do with who you are, what you want to be, or what you want to do. They are borrowed - more importantly, they are imposed. You never asked for these ideas. Thus, purifying the mind means recognizing that it is filled with ideas that have come from your strongest influences, which is the influence of your parents.

This is why Jesus says, "You cannot come to me if you cannot hate your parents." He goes a step further and says, "The one who identifies himself as the son of his mother and father will be called the son of a harlot." Because, according to him, your true mother and father are your own inner nature. You are a product of your own making. This is what yoga is about. It's about finding the source of your life, where you came from. If you accept another source, if you say, "I come from my parents," and try to live up to their expectations, you face a big contradiction. The level of courage, self-discipline, self-introspection, awareness, and intelligence required to walk such an arduous path becomes difficult if you start with the wrong assumption.

Jesus was not being rude when he said this. By stating that if you identify with your parents you would be called the son of a harlot, he's quite literally saying they are not your true parents. You came through them; they were only vehicles. They did not create you. You cannot be created. There is something inside you that is unborn, that can never take birth, that can never die. That is what you're trying to realize.

Spirituality is not mere child's play where you're just trying to know something more about your mind or your body. You are trying to go to the very heart of the matter: What is life? What is aliveness? What is consciousness? Will you live? Will you die? What is past life? What is future life? All the most important questions of life will be answered. How can you be stuck with such a simple, flimsy biological idea that you came from mortal flesh? Yes, your body came through it, but you are trying to understand if there is something more to you than just the body.

Purification starts with questioning these deeply entrenched ideas. You cannot address these things after you go inside; they are the obstacles that prevent you from beginning your inward journey. Why are you still on the outside? Why haven't you started your inward journey? These ideas have kept you comfortably asleep: "What is the necessity to find my own purpose? I already know what my purpose is. My purpose is to satisfy my father or my mother," so you don't feel the need to find your true purpose. "Where did I come from? Well, I came from my parents, and they came from their parents, so the lineage is clear. Why do I need to worry about birth and death?" That is what stops inquiry.

So, even before you turn inward, you must confront these ideas and the religious conditioning. Karl Marx said that religion was a symptom of a sick society, an opiate that made the diseased social system bearable and removed the will to find a cure by directing attention away from this world to the next. The very purpose of religion is to keep you crippled. The first thing religion does is break your legs and it does it in unawareness. You don't realize it. You're still learning about the world. You're still trying to understand what life is, what this religiousness is, what birth and death are. Religion cuts the source of that questioning. It claims you were created in someone else's image, and your purpose and destination are to satisfy that image.

What you do in this life determines whether you'll satisfy the one who created you or anger him. This is tantamount to breaking your legs. You are just beginning to walk. You still have so much to learn about walking, and then you have to run; you have to understand so much about your body. But your legs are broken. Now, for the rest of your life, you have accepted a subservient, diminished, and crippled version of yourself. That is why an individual who regards himself as truly free - intellectually, emotionally, physically - cannot be subservient to any religious ideas. Something inside will eat at him, something will clash. His own experiences will tell him that he is something different.

Only if one is able to recognize these influences can he stand on his own legs. It is hard because you've been made to believe that you don't have legs. Your search has been hijacked; your quest has been taken away. That is why it is really hard for a religious person, an individual who has accepted the dogmatic beliefs of his religion, to become a yogi. A yogi is a rebel by nature. If you cannot rebel against this deep-seated conditioning, you cannot walk the path of yoga. This is what is meant by purity - purifying your mind and your body, just clearing out the nonsense, pulling out the weeds, tilling the soil to keep it ready. Then, you can be ready for the next step, which is santosha or contentment.

SANTOSHA - CONTENTMENT

The next Niyama, or rule of discipline, that Patanjali introduces us to is santosha, or contentment. He states, "From an attitude of contentment, unexplained happiness, mental comfort, joy, and satisfaction are obtained." Perhaps this is the first time contentment is introduced not just as a result, but as a rule, as a discipline. Generally, it is assumed that contentment is a consequence - a result of accomplishing something. You cannot be content unless you have done something to reach that state. However, Patanjali suggests that you must cultivate contentment first to experience happiness, joy, and bliss that follow on the path of yoga.

Contentment is not an accomplishment or a consequence; it is a state. You either know how to be in that state, or you don't. In a way, what Patanjali is implying is that contentment cannot be taught. How can you teach contentment? At all times, there is something lacking in your life and something fulfilling you. It is impossible to be totally devoid of things that bring you joy and happiness. Even in moments of absolute despair or confusion, if you pay attention to what you have, you will find innumerable things that are there supporting you, holding you, cradling you in that very moment. Recognizing these things is essential.

Contentment involves becoming aware of the fact that there is something within you that does not need external support or justifications to exist. There is a part of you that is independent of your thinking. Your contentment is not linked to your thoughts. When your contentment is tied to your thought processes, that is not true contentment, but rather imagination. At every moment, there will always be things that you can call your own. Even when you're crying, you are still breathing. Your breath didn't stop and think, "This person is always crying; I should leave." So, what does this mean? Your suffering cannot take away your breath. No matter how much pain you're experiencing, no matter how unbearable, the vital forces of life are still with you. Breathing continues, digestion goes on, temperature regulation persists. If your body overheats, you will sweat to cool down. If you exert your body too much, you will sit down. Even when you're crying, if you suddenly see a snake, you will jump. You will not pick up the snake and let it bite you, thinking, "I'm so sad, I'm crying, it's okay, you can bite me." No. There are so many instinctual, natural forces supporting you. These things are yours, and nobody can take them away from you. That is why contentment cannot be taught - there is nothing lacking for you to experience contentment.

Yes, you need guidance to experience bliss, deeper states of joy, and deeper states of happiness because you have obscured these states with your imagination, your mind, and your thoughts. Since you are living in the world of thoughts, these deeper experiences remain invisible.

That is where a teacher comes in, because he knows and can see the things that are blocking you. He can guide you toward getting rid of them. This can be done for all deeper emotions, but contentment is your birthright. You are born with contentment. Only a part of you is searching. Only a part of you is disturbed at all times. There is another part of you that is deeply contented. In fact, this is one of the reasons why many people don't search for deeper experiences in life. At a certain level, they are contented. They don't see that something is really missing. They can go about their worldly activities and lose themselves in momentary pleasures of life, only because somewhere deep down, there is contentment.

Imagine for a moment that you had no way to connect with contentment. You would explode; you couldn't exist for even a single moment. Crying, pain, suffering - they're all easier to handle. But if you had no way of connecting with something stable, something of your own that you could be contented with, then you couldn't exist for even a moment. Your mind, body, and spirit would just explode. The reason you haven't yet exploded, the reason you are still alive and still identify suffering, pain, and joy, and say, "I am experiencing all these things," is because there is a part of you that is already settled. That's your basic framework of life, and it cannot be taken away from you. You have to accept contentment as a guiding principle; you cannot search for it.

Patanjali said that from an attitude of contentment, happiness, mental comfort, joy, and satisfaction are obtained. It is not a question of how much you possess. There is a common misunderstanding that ties contentment to the things we have or don't have. This is why people search for contentment in things, in experiences, in the outside world - because they have been conditioned to believe that by themselves, they are nothing; they are incomplete, useless, not worthy of attention, not worthy of love. They feel they must have something to be worthy. For example, there is a social construct that if you're homeless, you don't deserve love; if you live in a palace, you automatically receive it. This has nothing to do with your true self. You can be content being homeless or you can be chaotic living in a palace.

It is not about saying homelessness is superior to living in a palace, or vice versa. It's not a question of what you have; it's a question of accessing a state of mind that transcends your possessions. Whether you're homeless or living in a palace, you decide your state, you decide your level of contentment.

The reason this misunderstanding exists, and why people continue searching for contentment in things and experiences, is that this is what they have been taught from their upbringing. There is not a single moment when they have been appreciated simply for who they are. They have always been appreciated for what they have done, what they have accomplished, and what they have achieved. This pattern starts right from childhood. You don't typically go to a child and appreciate them just for being themselves. You don't give chocolates to a child when there is no special occasion. But when a child speaks for the first time, walks for the first time, or writes a letter for the first time, you appreciate and reward them more. "Oh, you did this today." And similarly, throughout their growing years, you celebrate milestones: "Oh, you finished one year of your schooling. What an accomplishment."

What this is doing is creating a deep-set conditioning where the child forgets all the innate qualities they are born with - intelligence, awareness, consciousness. Now, the child is only focused on those things that people are focusing on. As this continues, a day will come when an individual completely forgets to value the most important things that belong to them. Instead, they begin to only value those things for which they have to work, for which they have to put in effort, because it is only effort that is being appreciated by the world. Non-effort is not appreciated, yet contentment is non-effort; it inherently belongs to you.

The only way to truly understand and fully experience contentment is to disconnect it from possessions, to separate it from your activities. Yes, you will be appreciated for the things you do, especially if you can do something that is different and unique from those around you. The more different you are, the more the appreciation. However, contentment comes from recognizing those qualities that don't separate you but actually connect you to everything around you. Contentment comes from acknowledging qualities that are not unique to you, that people cannot identify as being possessed only by you. True contentment is recognizing the fundamental principles and forces of life that sustain everything. It is about being aware of the vast tapestry of life that supports you. It has nothing to do with what you have or don't have.

A Zen master says, "The master has no possessions." These "no possessions" may include a house, a car, a computer, a room full of books, and an electric toothbrush. He's not rejecting the comforts of life; he's not a nihilist. He does not hate comfort or possessing things. However, he does not base his contentment on the foundation of his possessions. That is the difference between someone who is intelligent enough to recognize his social conditioning and someone who is totally lost in it. Most people are simply lost in their social conditioning. They are not even aware of the treasures hidden within them. They do not realize that contentment is simply about being in the present moment and experiencing life as it is.

As Thich Nhat Hanh once beautifully put it, "Contentment is enjoying a non-toothache day." That's it. You are worried when you have a toothache, but when you don't have a toothache, are you rejoicing? No, you're probably worried about something else. Contentment is recognizing those things that are not broken, that will never be broken, that don't need fixing. Only a part of you is messed up. Even if you try to mess up your life completely from beginning to end, it's impossible. You can only interfere with certain aspects. Yes, you can interfere with your body. You can hurt your body. You can interfere with your mind. But there is something deep down inside you that you cannot touch, that does not belong to you, because that is you. You cannot grab hold of it and change it. Contentment belongs to that space.

Now, why is it important to be content on the journey toward discovering your true nature? What is actually happening is simply a deepening of that contentment. You need to understand what contentment is in order to deepen and expand it. This possibility must be recognized because it is not something new. Everything you experience on the journey of yoga, on the journey of meditation, you have already experienced at some level. If you experience joy, you know what joy is. If you experience bliss, you also know what bliss is. These are familiar experiences that you will encounter again and again, with one significant difference: now you are moving toward them consciously. Your world, your universe, is becoming more and more filled with these things that you are seeking. Nothing new is being added to your being; you are only being reintroduced to those things that already belong to you.

If you don't recognize these things at least at some level, you might not be fully contented with your life, which is natural. That is why you want to understand more about yourself. But if you know nothing about contentment, then you cannot even begin your journey - it is that measure of intellectual settling that you identify as contentment which eventually becomes existential settling.

At a certain intuitive level, you should at least recognize that you are contented. Otherwise, how can you sit in meditation? How can you focus? How can you be aware? If you're not contented, you will constantly be looking for things on the outside to fill that void, making it impossible to be still or silent. You won't be able to recognize the value of silence and stillness because they are simply introducing you to the contentment that's already there within you, expanding it and making you more aware of it.

What happens when you sit and watch your breath? You're not creating the breath. You're not altering the breath. You are merely recognizing the breath - the simplicity, purity, and silence of it - to eventually realize, "When I'm stressed, worried, or anxious, I have a place to go. It is right here. My own breath. My breath never scolds me; it never insults me. It is always there. When I am suffering, my breath is not suffering. Yes, its rhythm may change a bit just so that I can recognize what's happening, but my breath is always peaceful." Contentment opens up the possibility of greater contentment, greater joy, happiness, and bliss.

TAPAS - BURNING DESIRE

The next Niyama that Patanjali talks about is tapas, or austerity. He says, "Through self-discipline and austerity, one gains mastery over the body and the senses." This is another unusual rule, or niyama. Tapas, often understood as penance or austerity, is generally assumed to encapsulate what yoga is. When a yogi sits in meditation, longing to become something more, longing to become himself, that process is identified as tapas.

For example, when I started sitting in meditation, it was a complete shock to my family members. They could not reconcile the idea of me sitting still; I have always been active. I remember my mother, who has been around kids as a teacher, telling stories about me. She said I was the most difficult kid she ever handled because I would not sit still. I was always restless. You couldn't leave me anywhere near a tree because the next moment I'd be climbing it. Many of the injuries and scars I have are from falling out of trees. The only time I was at rest is when I was asleep. If I wasn't asleep, I was active.

Now here I was, sitting in meditation for hours, sometimes the entire day. They're puzzled, wondering what was happening. They used the word "tapas." They'd say, "Oh, he's actually sitting in tapas." They didn't say I was sitting in meditation because typically, when you meditate, you sit for a while and then you get up. But I didn't want to get up. I seized every opportunity to sit, and I would only get up when it was absolutely necessary - to eat, to move around and stretch, to attend to certain tasks. Otherwise, I was perfectly content to simply sit.

They started telling themselves and people around them that I was actually going into tapas, which was unusual. Fortunately for me, they had been introduced to the idea that if you disturb a person who's sitting in tapas, you will go to hell. This belief is deeply rooted in Indian culture. You never disturb someone who is in tapas. We've heard all kinds of stories about the consequences of disturbing someone's tapas - how the disturber was condemned to live the rest of their lives in pain, suffering, and misery. So, they never disturbed me while I was sitting in meditation.

All the disturbance came when I got up - that's when they would argue, fight, and question me. "Why are you sitting for such a long time?" But the moment I sat, they would fall silent. For me, that became another refuge. Instead of arguing with them, trying to convince them - which they likely wouldn't understand anyway - I realized that while I was sitting in meditation, they wouldn't disturb me. So, I started sitting more.

Tapas is a burning desire and marks the beginning of your yogic journey, not the end or the middle. It's a longing that you bring to your search, a longing that knows no bounds, no limitations, and is unconcerned about time or people. When your mind seizes a strong, existential desire to know itself, you are in the grip of that desire and you become a yogi. That moment of intense desire is what separates a yogi from someone lost in samsara - the cyclic existence of life, birth, and death. Samsara is moving from one thought to another, one idea to another, seeking meaning and justification for your actions by observing the actions of those around you. That is samsara. In samsara, you understand your life based on the lives of people around you, reflecting and thinking based on what others say is right or wrong.

In tapas, you completely cut off the outside. The desire to be, the desire to know yourself, is so deep and strong that you are literally burning with desire. Nobody will dare come close to that burning intensity. And you know these moments when you are so sure about something, when your desire is so strong, you have no trouble holding on to it. In fact, the universe itself clears the path. It recognizes the yogic quality in you, and the moment it sees that, the universe signals, "Don't mess with him. Don't mess with her. She is possessed by something deeper, something greater." People will understand that too.

Whether you're sitting in meditation or not, whether your body is in a recognizable yogic posture or not, your internal tapas - that austerity - can be recognized. It shows in your words, your actions, and the way you think. This cannot be cultivated; you have to find it. How can you cultivate a burning desire? It isn't a gradual process. It's an explosion that just happens. Suddenly, you realize this is your life's purpose. This is what you want to do. Everything else moves to the periphery, and that one desire occupies the central space. It becomes the most important thing around which your life will now revolve, and you can see this without any problem. All other desires are still there, but they've moved far away to the edges. That one central, burning desire has taken hold of you. A yogi is someone who has been possessed by this burning desire.

There is another beautiful Sanskrit word, "tapasvi" - the one who has become tapas itself. He is not merely trying to be austere; he is not in a state of panic; he is not doing penance. He *is* penance. He is a tapasvi. He is a yogi. He has become that yearning, that burning desire, so much so that he himself - his mind, his body, his actions, his thought processes - have all become subservient to that central burning desire. It is a moment when something takes center stage. Up until now, his center was occupied by thoughts and desires. Now, for the first time, all those are pushed aside, and a new burning desire - a longing to know oneself - has risen inside. That is tapas, the starting point of a yogic journey.

SVADHYAYA - SELF-STUDY

Svadhyaya, or self-study and self-reflection, involves the study of scriptures and yourself, enabling you to develop communion with your chosen deity or idea. Patanjali emphasizes this as an indispensable rule that you must embrace unconditionally if you are to walk the path of self-realization. This involves understanding intellectually and deciphering for yourself, using your intelligence and ability to discern between right and wrong, good and bad. You supply the most important ingredient for the inward journey: understanding. It is your intellectual understanding that eventually becomes your experiential understanding. You're not going to find something totally different from what you're searching for. You have to know what you're looking for; otherwise, how can you travel on the path?

Yoga is not a blind dash toward a destination; it is a systematic, step-by-step descent into the depths of your being. You must know your steps, recognize the signs of this descent, and also be aware when you are stumbling, making mistakes, or going in circles. This level of awareness is only possible when your intellectual understanding is not only ripe but also precise, clear, and correct. If your intellectual understanding of life, the nature of reality, and the mind and body are not aligned, then your inward journey will be fraught with contradictions because you won't clearly know what you're looking for.

Studying scriptures is as important as practicing yoga. Intellectual understanding is as essential as experiential exploration. It is indispensable. In fact, it is ultimately your intellectual understanding that transforms into your experiential realization.

You already know what you're looking for, at least in the mental realm. More importantly, you know what you're not looking for, and that knowledge keeps you on the path. It is this knowledge that gives you the power to discern what you are seeking and what you are trying to avoid. That is why, since the beginning of time, wherever you find written scriptures, you will find spiritual knowledge. Some of the oldest scriptures are dedicated to the spiritual understanding of life. They are not accounts of social conversations, tax collection documents, or descriptions of daily life. The most significant and oldest documents record an individual's search for truth, his quest for something higher, something beyond.

For example, one of the oldest known scriptures, dating back to around 3500 BC - over three millennia before Jesus and older than the Vedas or the Hebrew Bible - is dedicated to a king's search for immortality. The Epic of Gilgamesh is recorded on cuneiform tablets and details this king's quest for immortality. Similarly, the Egyptian Book of the Dead, which can be dated to the second millennium BC, is another of the oldest scriptures. It is dedicated to helping a deceased individual navigate the dream realm to meet his final judgment.

What this actually implies is that there is an afterlife, a life beyond death. An individual needs to understand what that life will be like. They need to comprehend the dream realm and be aware of the consequences of their actions. They must know their mind and body well. Judgment comes from within, not from a deity sitting externally, judging your actions. After death, your mind is reduced to its basic functions; your physical body is gone. Only a self-image of you, your pure self, and remnants of your mind and body to judge your actions remain. Your intellectual understanding of life aids you in this process.

Egyptians believed that a pharaoh needed this knowledge for his afterlife. Therefore, scriptures written on papyrus scrolls were buried with the deceased to accompany them on their journey. If scriptures are deemed useful in the afterlife, one can only imagine their importance in this life: They are indispensable.

A human being is distinct because he can read and write, understand scriptures, and thus travel back through time to connect with civilizations, human societies, and their cultures. Everything we know about our past comes from the scriptures. This gives an enormous sense of meaning, purpose, and richness to human life, which is absent in animals. In terms of physical and mental abilities, a human being is not dramatically different from other animals.

What is that one thing that separates humans from animals? Humans have an awareness and understanding of their past. They can discuss a human who lived three thousand years ago. An animal, however, cannot remember anything beyond the last few days of its experiences. This limited understanding and awareness of life is not because animals are inferior; it's because they do not have a culture preserved in language, no scriptures to guide them. This lack of symbolic notation cuts off their higher search. If animals had symbolic notations, their search would not be so limited. In fact, animals are as capable of enlightenment as humans if only we could understand and communicate with them in their own language, introducing them to deeper spiritual understanding. It's not impossible, but they are isolated in this regard.

There are numerous examples of animals learning language. Coco, the gorilla, could communicate using sign language, easily forming words, sentences, and even complex ideas. If you can teach an animal to this extent, introducing it to inner emotions and feelings, then introducing it to the subtler realms of silence and stillness is merely a matter of teaching. The situation is similar in human communities. Most people are not even aware of the existence of inner silence; silence and stillness are alien concepts unless they have been introduced to them. Unless they have been exposed to spiritual scriptures that symbolically decode the deeper realms of life, they remain stuck at an intellectual level. Our ability to read and write, to record and revisit our collective knowledge - the reservoir of wisdom we recognize as spiritual - is what can help us awaken to our highest nature. It's all contained within those few symbolic notations.

A seeker on the path must decipher the symbolic language of spirituality for himself. The way he understands these words, the earnestness with which he interprets them, and the sharpness with which he deciphers them determine whether he can understand what's happening internally. Yes, experientially, there's still a long way to go, but intellectually, one must start seeing things in the right way. Now, why do I emphasize the "right way"? What is missing in your daily experiences of life? In daily life, existence is broken down into concepts and ideas to facilitate navigation. We don't understand existence for what it truly is. We don't fully grasp the nature of the body or the mind. We are far from the correct understanding of life; we are closer to a convenient understanding of life.

Although we are constantly surrounded by language - talking and listening all the time - most of it is not wisdom or knowledge, it's just empty noise. One thing is described in terms of another. What is light? Light makes things visible, that's the definition of light. Well, I know that light makes things visible because when there's no light, it's dark, and things aren't visible, but you haven't given me a profound explanation. What is light? It illuminates things. I know that, but that's where our understanding stops.

We don't want to admit that we don't truly know what light, darkness, clouds, stars, a human body, or a mind is. Yet, we have concepts for all of these. And what do we really know about these? We just have a way of identifying them, separating them from the rest. What is a fruit? It's not a leaf. What is a leaf? It's not a branch. What is a branch? It's not a tree. What is a tree? It's not the earth. That's our explanation. We don't actually understand anything. But in the world of language, it seems like we know so much.

Human beings are so smart, so intelligent. Take the smartest human being and put him in the wild - you will see how "smart" he really is. He wouldn't survive a day because he's living in a world created by and for himself to satisfy his own ego. If a man is truly knowledgeable, then he should be able to survive anywhere; he should be adaptable. Most human beings would fail the nature test because you cannot use your mathematics, science, philosophy, or religion in nature. If you don't know that you're eating a poisonous leaf, you simply don't know - that's going to be the end of your story. Your intellectual knowledge is useless there.

So, you have to start with the assumption that you know nothing. Your knowledge is useless for navigating the inner dimensions of life. Your so-called wealth of knowledge is meaningless when you want to be a yogi. That breaking point, that separation between your false knowledge and the beginning of acquiring true knowledge, is what makes a yogi. That is what yoga is - it's a way of looking at things.

Going back to the word "yoga," which means "union," you cannot chop things up to understand them. That is the basic definition of yoga: either you know something in its totality, or you know nothing about it. Take a tree, for example. Ask anyone what a tree is, and the only way they typically describe it is in terms of names and classifications: This tree belongs to this species, this genus; it has this type of leaves and produces such and such fruit. But when I ask a simple question - what is a tree? - there's no explanation.

If you were to ask the same question in yoga, you must give an answer before going inward. Otherwise, what are you searching for on the inside? What is a tree? You have to either admit that you know nothing about the tree, or you might say, "It is an experience. For me, it is just an experience of colors, of movement. Now, what is the difference between a rock and a tree? A tree moves. A rock sits still. At least perceptually, that is how I see it. If I see a rock, a tree, and a human being, one thing I can identify is this gradation in movement. A human moves more than a tree; a tree moves more than a rock. That's as much as I know." So, you're breaking down life into basic experiences. You are not overlaying it with your concepts, your ideas, or your theories, because in yoga, everything is connected, and it is connected to you.

There are no independent realities out there; everything is one extension. Let's say, for example, that you can intellectually explore, understand, and come to certain conclusions. You conclude that you are not your mind and you are not your body. This is a simple understanding that you can arrive at intellectually. Now, why am I not my mind? Well, I can use my mind. I can stop a thought, alter a thought, play with my mind, and watch my mind. Similarly with my body - I can see my hand move. Now my body is sitting here, but I can make it move.

I can make a decision that will alter the position or the shape of this body. What does that mean? That means I am not my body. How can I be my body and still move it? This simple understanding leads to the realization that I must be something different. I don't know what that is, but at least I can assert that I am not my mind, I'm not my body.

In yoga, each of these understandings can eventually become your ultimate reality. So, if you hold on to this understanding, if you have explored this idea thoroughly, read enough scriptures, and compared the spiritual scriptures from different cultures and understandings, you will eventually arrive at the intellectual conclusion that you are not your mind, you are not your body. This understanding supports concepts like reincarnation, discussions about life extending beyond death, and notions of free will because you are recognized as something more than just your mind and body. Enlightened beings have spoken about the self as the ultimate reality, not the mind and the body. This realization then becomes your tool, your companion on your inner journey. You cannot embark on this journey blindly; this understanding lights your way.

Yoga is not like a university where you go to explore and earn your PhD; rather, you need to have your PhD - in terms of understanding life - before you even begin. Without this, you will be clueless and alone when you go inward. Your teacher and guidance are on the outside, while you are left facing the vast unknown of your being all alone. And what are you armed with? If it's nothing, you'll be metaphorically chopped to pieces. You'll be so disoriented, confused, and lost that you'll come running back to the surface, not understanding what's happening because you're not looking for anything specific. You haven't acquired enough knowledge to use as guidance.

Let's say you conclude that the ultimate purpose of life is to fully know life - a simple statement that will be completed on your yogic journey. What am I trying to experience? I'm not trying to experience something outside of myself. I'm not trying to see an image of a person. I'm trying to fully understand life. What does that statement do? It helps you stay on the path until your understanding of life becomes complete. Otherwise, somewhere in the middle, you might conclude that you already know enough. It is your intellectual understanding that guides you internally.

Life is a dream. Death is an illusion. Self is the ultimate reality. Self is Nirguna Brahman. What are these concepts? They are your companions on your inward journey, especially when you're confused or uncertain about what's happening inside. When you've been waiting for something to happen and nothing has, what will you use? These ideas. When you say, "Self is Nirguna Brahman," what does that mean? It means the Self has no qualities. As long as there are qualities attributed, I still haven't found my true self. If I am saying, "I am relaxed, I am peaceful, I am blissful," then I am not Nirguna Brahman. I am still entangled in thoughts. What does this mean? It means I must continue on my journey.

Intellectual understanding is where you become a yogi, where you become a meditator. And this intellectual understanding must continue throughout your journey. You must continue to read and study the scriptures. You must continue to supplement your experiential journey with intellectual understanding. This ongoing study helps you see where you're headed. It's by comparing your journey to the journeys of those who have traveled before you that you gain necessary signs and indications of progress on your path.

A scripture is a text that originates from those who have embarked on a profound inward journey, navigating the inner realms of the mind and the body. These texts offer insights not just into intellectual concepts or ideas, but into deep spiritual experiences. This is why the study of spiritual scriptures is distinct from the study of intellectual concepts - it's about traversing through the minds of those who have traveled these paths before.

Intellectual understanding of spiritual scriptures involves navigating through the insights and wisdom of those who have genuinely experienced and understood these deeper realities - it's not just about theoretical knowledge or concepts discussed in classrooms and universities. The knowledge shared by those who have merely conceptualized ideas without true experiential understanding can be limited when it comes to the inward journey.

To effectively use spiritual scriptures for your own spiritual growth, you must be able to discern that the teachings you study come from an awakened, illumined mind - a mind that has traversed the entire path to enlightenment. You don't need to be extraordinarily smart to discern this; you simply need to have read enough to recognize the difference between mere intellectual knowledge and true experiential wisdom. While you are acquiring this knowledge intellectually, the essence of what you learn must be deeply experiential. This ensures that the scripture you engage with truly aids in your spiritual journey, offering more than just intellectual stimulation but also guiding you toward real transformation and self-realization.

"Life is a dream." No philosopher can say this. No scientist can say this. No preacher can say this. The source of that statement is an experiential understanding. An individual has actually seen that life is a dream. Buddha can say that life is a dream. He says you are nothing but your mind. Death is an illusion. A scientist cannot say death is an illusion. A religious person cannot say death is an illusion. For him, death is real. In fact, his whole business starts after death. Who can make such a statement? Only the one who has conquered death, the one who has faced death, the one who has triumphed over death. Only an enlightened person can say death is an illusion. You only have to ensure that the source is the ultimate source. That helps you to trust the knowledge, trust the wisdom. And then if you find the same knowledge in multiple places, from multiple experiential sources, that becomes your intellectual framework. Now, the more you study the scriptures, the more you understand intellectually. You are now only waiting for all that intellectual understanding to ripen, deepen, and become an experiential understanding.

Your mind knows what you are searching for; now it's time for the body to understand it. Yoga is that simple. You conceptually introduce truth to the mind. The mind should long for it, search for it, and go on an inward pilgrimage in pursuit of it. Eventually, the body is what realizes it experientially. What are life, death, birth, pain, and suffering? Only the body can understand these things intuitively, and experientially, while the mind can comprehend them intellectually. Yoga is the transformation of the body.

There will come a moment in your yogic journey when this wisdom will simply distill. Your body will suddenly awaken to all these realities. In a single moment, all these intellectual understandings will explode into experiential knowing. That is why one of the important niyamas is self-study - so that you can rely on your own understanding on the inward journey. Ishvara pranidhana, or surrender to the divine, leads to samadhi and the realization of the true self by surrendering to the divine within.

What does Patanjali mean by surrender to the divine? What divine is he talking about? Is it god? Is it your religious god? Is it an idea of god that you have in your mind, because if you surrender to the wrong god, you are screwed. You don't have to go far to see how people have messed themselves up by surrendering to the wrong gods. They think they have surrendered to God, but they only surrendered to Man's ego. Religious surrendering is surrendering to Man's ego. Man has cleverly disguised his ego as God. You will not find Jesus in Christianity. You will not find Buddha in Buddhism. You will only find human ego disguised in their names. Their true teachings are hidden somewhere. So what divine? What is he talking about? He's talking about equality. He's talking about something higher that you cannot see, that you cannot experience, that is guiding everything.

Your self-study and intellectual understanding will help you see this. There is so much happening. But how can all this occur without intelligence, without awareness, without consciousness? That is what Patanjali refers to as the divine - something higher, a power above and beyond your understanding; not a person, not a human being, not a fixed entity. Something that permeates the entire universe. That is what you are trying to surrender to.

Now, why is surrender important? It is crucial because you are your biggest obstacle. Your ego is your biggest obstacle. You are holding on to a false self-image and refusing to let go. Surrendering helps you to let go. It need not even be a surrender to the divine; surrender to something other than your ego - surrender to a stone or a tree; it is equivalent to surrendering to the divine.

Patanjali speaks of the divine because, during his time, people were deeply religious - there weren't many atheists back then. Religion was a very important and integral part of their lives. He uses the concept of a religious deity to facilitate surrender because that was what they believed in. For the modern person, surrender could be to an imaginary force, to consciousness, to aliveness, or something existential. What is important is not what you are surrendering to, but that you are surrendering, because the inner journey is a journey of surrender. Only when you surrender, only when you let go, can you descend to the depths of your being. You cannot cling to your self-image or your ego and navigate the unknown realms of your being.

Hence, surrendering is another guiding principle on your journey. **Surrender, self-study, contentment, tapas,** and **purity:** Simple guidelines that will become your eternal companions on your yogic journey. This is your basic foundation. These are the limbs with which you will move. These are the foundations. The deeper your understanding of these niyamas, these rules, the more steadfast and disciplined you are in practicing them, the easier your journey becomes. You have to spend more time with these basic rules or niyamas than doing anything else. There is no need to hurry.

Patanjali next goes to the inward journey. He talks about focus, dharana, and dhyana meditation. But these niyamas should be revisited again and again. This is not just a step you take and move forward.

This is a constant step that you carry with you. As long as you are searching, these rules will help you align your search. Simple rules, simple guidelines, that will help you experience the profound.

ASANA - PERFECT POSTURE

Everything you're searching for, the answers to all your questions, lies in a single experience - that moment when your outward understanding provides a clear vision, showing that the path inward is the only way. You're seeking just one moment. No matter how long it takes, how much effort you must exert, or how much discomfort, pain, and misery you must endure, what you're looking for is a single explosive moment that reveals the true nature of who you are, the true nature of reality. You can name this experience however you wish: awakening, enlightenment, self-realization, Nirvana, or the desire to transcend mind and body, to forget oneself. You can use positive or negative words to describe this experience. "Nirvana" is a negative term, meaning "blowing out" or "extinguishing." Yet, it signifies an ultimate experience that is anything but negative.

You have understood the world of ideas and concepts, and you know where it leads. You understand the purpose of a worldly journey, of education, going to work, getting married, and having children. You've seen the game that is played on the outside and know without any doubt that there are no answers there. What you're searching for is within. You are essentially looking for a single moment, one moment that can complete you. This is the starting point of yoga, the beginning of turning inward. Now, how do you undertake this inward journey? What physical posture should you assume? What are the dos and don'ts of this posture?

YOGASANA

Patanjali gives us our cue. While the world has almost forgotten the distinction between yoga and asana, often calling it a single phenomenon, "yogasana," in reality, there is no such thing as "yogasana." There is yoga, and there is asana, which helps you explore and understand yoga. Yogasana itself is not a practice. Unfortunately, most people know yoga as physical exercise; they think yoga is gymnastics. Yoga has nothing to do with the body. The body is merely a prop, a device, a method, a tool. The entire focus and attention of yoga are on the mind, on transforming the mind. The emphasis is on the philosophy of understanding, navigating the subtler realms of the mind, understanding the subtler sensations of the body, to reach the subtlest of realities - the self, which illuminates everything, is at the center of all your experiences, and is the destination of your search.

Now, why have we deviated so far from the actual meaning and purpose of yoga? Why do we think of physical exercises when we hear the term "yoga," especially in the West? For the Western mind, yoga and meditation are seen as two completely different things, when in fact, they are one and the same. Yoga simply provides a broader framework, but ultimately, the objective is meditation and mindfulness, and the purpose of yoga is the purpose of meditation: to help you become enlightened, to awaken from the sleep of life.

So, where did we falter? What went wrong? It's important to understand that human beings are mostly visual creatures. We place enormous emphasis on what we see - so much so, that our actual experiences hardly matter as long as something looks good, intriguing, and engaging. Our attention is drawn toward it, and this is how life has remained a mystery for such a long time. Despite conscious individuals searching for the meaning of life for centuries, the general population still has no conception of what life truly is. Life remains a total mystery to philosophers, scientists, religious people - to everyone. When in fact, the truth is not somewhere far away; it is staring us right in the face. What you're searching for is so close to you. You're searching for yourself. There's not a single moment you are separated from it, and yet, you are totally oblivious to the realm of reality because you have become a creature of appearance. You believe only what you see. You have forgotten how to trust your experiences, and how to connect with the subtler dimensions. In fact, you call it "subtle" because you have attached yourself to the gross visual dimension.

If you're sitting and people-watching, two things are happening. First, your mind is recording changes - something is moving, and that's where your attention is drawn. But in that very moment, you are also silent, still, and there is a breath flowing in its own quiet rhythm, of which you are totally unaware. Simply close your eyes, and you will become aware of all this. Just closing your eyes, an act that requires no effort, redirects your attention back to the body. Observing your breath becomes much easier with your eyes closed than with them open.

What does this mean? It means that the world of illusions is sustained by our visual senses. What we see covers up the truth. The colors, the lights, the shadows, the movement - these are our fascinations. That is why we are fascinated with the physical form of the body, why we are captivated by doing something with the body. While the true purpose is internal transformation, we cling to outward changes.

Yoga postures are designed to bring your awareness to the unchanging essence within, using the body as a contrast where change is evident. In every yoga posture you take, every asana you assume, if you are fully aware while adopting that posture, you can observe that only a small part of you is changing. The majority of what you recognize as you - your aliveness, your consciousness, your being - remains untouched. Whether you stand on your feet or your head, you are still you. Your soul is not upside down; your spirit is not turned over. Your world remains as it was. Consider the simplicity of this idea.

If you were to close your eyes, connect with your breath, and enter a state of meditative silence, it would not matter whether you were standing on your head or your feet. In the internal realm, the physical form has no influence, despite the significant meaning you attach to it. That is the purpose of a posture - to show a student, to demonstrate to a disciple that you can twist your body however you want, but you cannot twist your spirit. Your spirit is untwistable. Why? Because it is an unchanging reality. It is so pure, so complete that the physicality of life doesn't even touch it, let alone diminish or harm it.

Because we are fascinated with the body and its form, and because we are interested in recording the experiences of the body, yoga becomes another avenue of entertainment. This happens because you can see yourself doing something that you normally don't do. It takes effort to assume those postures, and the mind is fascinated with effort - it satisfies the ego. "I was able to do mastakasana. I was able to do matsyasana." Different names, different experiences - it feels good. It feels like you're making progress every day. But in reality, you are only twisting yourself more and more.

Consider the animal kingdom: almost every creature has a yogic posture dedicated to it. There are hundreds and hundreds of yoga postures, each dedicated to one creature. You can "meditate like a frog" or "like a snake." It's still meditation, but we are overly concerned with the physical form. Internally, you are supposed to meditate on the formless, yet you're so obsessed with the form that you forget to go inward. You move from one asana to another, never pausing to explore each posture's deeper, underlying purpose.

STHIRA SUKHAM ASANAM

In Patanjali's Yoga Sutras, which outlines the eight limbs of yoga, only a couple of lines are dedicated to asana. He defines asana simply as "a steady, comfortable posture." His exact words are "sthira sukham asanam," which translates to "Posture should be steady and comfortable." Where then, are the gymnastics? Where is the twisting? Where are all the different animal postures you can assume? Where is the torturing? Nowhere to be found in his sutras.

Patanjali's definition is clear: "sthira" is firm, "sukham" is comfortable, and "asana" is essentially to sit. He's advising us to sit in a comfortable posture. That's it. There, according to Patanjali, ends your practice and the discussion of asana. What happens internally is what yoga truly is, and underscores the major misunderstanding between yoga as a philosophy, a way of life, a method of transcendence, and yoga merely as a physical exercise or a means of relaxation. Yes, there are some benefits to yogasana - it keeps your body flexible and helps the basic functionalities of the body to align themselves. You cannot perform these yogic exercises if you're not healthy or if you're not fit. If you're overweight or sick, you would struggle to engage in yoga. Thus, these postures can be useful to gauge your level of outward physical health.

The usefulness of yogasanas does not end there, but their role should not be overemphasized. As long as you are aware that yogasanas are simply one aspect of yoga - an exercise - and do not confuse it with the deeper, meditative aspects of yoga, it's alright. Yoga, in its fullest expression, transcends physical activity and touches on deeper spiritual and existential realms.

Confusion arises when people engage in gymnastics and think that they are practicing yoga, calling themselves yogis. In reality, they are more akin to contortionists. A true yogi is someone who searches for the ultimate truth, someone striving to merge their mind, body, and the universe into one unified whole. This is the essence of the word "yoga." A yogi continuously seeks to fuse experiences, searching for that singular experience that can complete him. He is not concerned with achieving a headstand, the fish meditation posture, or how he looks while assuming a yogic pose. He is not interested in capturing pictures to display on social media.

For a yogi, such physical postures are merely distractions from his true quest. This is why Patanjali defines the ideal yogic posture simply as sthira sukham asanam - a posture that is steady and comfortable. This is what your yogic posture should be, emphasizing the inner experience over the external form.

Asana in yoga is essentially about finding a posture that combines firmness and comfort. Imagine you're setting out on a journey, boarding a bus for a hundred-mile trip. What posture would you assume for this long journey? Would you opt for a headstand, or would you simply sit? This analogy highlights the difference between performative yogic gymnastics and assuming a comfortable posture suitable for extended periods.

In yoga, you are a traveler with a long path ahead. This journey is intuitive and calls for common sense; it doesn't require much effort to understand that a comfortable posture is essential because the journey is extensive. If your aim is merely a short stint, like a ten-minute bus ride, then perhaps experimenting with complex postures like a headstand could seem fitting. But often, this misses the broader point: you have forgotten that yoga is a journey, a long inward journey, not an outward performance.

Forgetting that the easiest way to journey inward is by keeping the outward comfortable can lead to distractions; your attention should not be drawn away by discomfort. Being firm in your posture helps keep you awake and alert. If you are too relaxed and not sufficiently firm, you risk falling asleep, which isn't the goal. You want to be fully present and aware of where you're going. This journey is not only exciting but also deeply revealing. Each moment on this meditative journey offers new insights and discoveries. Thus, lying down unconsciously is not considered a yogic posture. Sitting comfortably yet alertly bridges the practice of meditation and yoga, making them indistinguishable. Each posture should support awareness and engagement with the journey, emphasizing that the process is as significant as the destination.

A yogi, more often than not, is found sitting still, comfortably yet firmly. This firmness reflects their attentiveness to the inner journey they are observing. The comfort, referred to as "sukham" in Sanskrit, is equally crucial. Why is comfort necessary? If you are not comfortable, say, if you are sitting on a bed of nails, would you be able to appreciate the sunset? Would you notice the birds or be open to observing what's happening around you? Likely not. Your entire focus would be consumed by the discomfort, the feeling of that single nail piercing your skin.

When you are uncomfortable, your attention is diverted to managing that discomfort, rather than being free to explore or engage with deeper experiences, whether internal or external. For a yogi, being comfortable means eliminating unnecessary distractions that pull attention away from the inward journey. The goal is to cultivate a state where the physical posture is no longer a source of distraction but rather a stable foundation that supports deeper exploration and awareness. This is why comfort in posture is emphasized - it allows the yogi to maintain focus on the spiritual aspects of their practice, observing and participating in the journey without external interference.

The purpose of yoga is to shift attention from the outside to the inside. If your body is comfortable and not demanding attention, that is when the inward journey begins and relaxation occurs. Much misunderstanding arises because many have missed the most important aspect of yoga: it is an inward journey. The moment you recognize it as a journey, all the torturing of the body, pushing it to the limits of comfort, starving it, and twisting it into extreme postures, appears unnecessary.

Yogasana, practiced as extreme physical exertion, can be like torture. The body naturally resists unnatural positions; hands, legs, head, and torso are comfortable in their typical positions and are not interested in being forced into unfamiliar ones. This is why it takes time - months, or even years of practice to master these postures. Furthermore, those who focus excessively on perfecting their physical postures might forget to travel inward and enjoy the scenery. They miss the most important aspects of what yoga truly is about.

I once met a so-called yogi, a famous one, who was revered and loved by his community. Someone suggested that I should visit this yogi. It had been nearly a year since I started my meditation journey, and I was immersed in a world of my own. My entire understanding of life had changed - what is important and what is not - because I had already begun to experience life in a totally different way. From my external experiences, I could see that most of what we do on the outside is simply to lead us inward. The inward journey is the most crucial thing. Yet this person insisted, claiming there was something unique about this yogi. He's the most famous yogi in our region, and he thought our meeting would be fascinating because this yogi does not talk about meditation. At that moment, I sensed something was off. He probably called himself a yogi but was famous for other reasons. Still, he insisted, "No, he does not talk about meditation, awakening, or enlightenment, but he's a great yogi. He's loved and revered." And since he lived about twenty minutes from where I was staying, I decided to go and meet him.

I went to his place, and his assistant directed me to sit on a chair, mentioning that the master was in the garden and would join me shortly. Meanwhile, he handed me an album, and I wondered why he was giving me an album. I wanted to meet the "yogi." Handing out the album was their routine for every visitor. This album showcased all the yogic postures the yogi had assumed, filled with contortions, twists, and the accolades he had received. Essentially, it was marketing material for the yogi, illustrating how many people attended his last session and his popularity. Everywhere in the house, there were pictures of him in various yogic postures, setting a specific atmosphere. I flipped through the photographs, then set them aside and began waiting. Soon after, the yogi appeared, and with his assistant standing by, we began to talk.

After about ten minutes, he instructed his assistant to leave the room. The assistant, his devoted disciple who handled all the marketing and tended to the master's needs, was visibly surprised and hesitant but eventually left. Alone now, the yogi locked the door, approached me, and fell at my feet, confessing, "I know nothing about yoga. I have wasted my whole life. I am not enlightened. I've never truly journeyed inward." This revelation seemed to stem from our initial conversation which had impacted him deeply - perhaps because he had never before connected the physical aspects of yoga with its mental and spiritual dimensions. He broke down in tears, lamenting, "What have I done with my life? Nobody told me this. Nobody explained that yogasana is a form of meditation, a way of understanding something deeper." He was quite distraught, reflecting on a life spent pursuing recognition without grasping the true essence of the teachings he professed to follow. "Now here you are, I cannot even comprehend what you're talking about, but I know that is what I'm searching for. And I know that is what I have been searching for. But I didn't know it."

That is the so-called physical yogasana. There are hundreds and hundreds of people, thousands of people who regard themselves as yogis just because they know how to twist their bodies. There are people who appreciate that because they cannot do it. This, however, is not the goal of yoga. Suggesting such a thing is like reducing something profound to something trivial - it's like a child being even more childish. We must be mindful of the childlike aspect within us because, deep down, we are all somewhat childlike, lacking a deep understanding of life. Subtler aspects of life hold little importance to the childlike mindset, which prefers to play, turning anything and everything into a game.

This playful tendency has even transformed yogic postures - a simple method of connecting inward - into an exciting, outwardly focused activity. Consequently, it has become merely an activity of the body, disconnected from the mind, causing the true essence of yoga to be easily lost.

Unless you are introduced to the correct understanding of yoga, and unless your yogic journey is supplemented with knowledge - reading the scriptures and viewing it as a cleansing process both inside and out - you will miss the whole point. It is a great tragedy to start the journey and then stop midway without even realizing that you have stopped. For years, you might continue doing something, thinking you are making progress, thinking you are evolving, but in reality, your journey halted the moment you became obsessed with the physical body and started identifying yourself with the praise that the body was receiving.

A yogi is a warrior, a ferocious lion, who does not seek appreciation or accolades. His destination is the ultimate. The moment you started identifying yourself with the body and its capabilities because it found meaning and purpose in the appreciation of others, you veered off the path. From practicing yoga, you inadvertently turned into someone utterly disconnected from its true purpose.

I could see the pain in that man's eyes because he had indeed put tremendous effort into learning all those yogic postures. He had mastered them all. Perfecting those postures takes enormous amounts of time and energy. He had consulted books, gone deeply into the mechanics of each pose, and perfected his technique. That was why he was recognized as a famous yogi. But upon realizing that he had missed the entire purpose of yoga, you could see the confusion now compounded within him. What was he to do with all this knowledge and skill?

Now, he faced the daunting task of surrendering all that he had learned, of letting go to truly turn inward. Yet, he had already built an empire around his physical abilities - what would happen to that? What about his disciple, who had devoted himself to marketing these skills? Imagine going to that disciple and telling him that all this is useless, that there's no need to market anymore, that there's nothing here to market. This is the predicament of a body that has forgotten the mind, a body that has lost touch with its true nature - a body that is merely a body.

Yoga is about recognizing that the body is the least useful aspect of your inward journey. It should simply be placed in a position where it does not demand all your attention - it's a subtle art. While your journey starts with the body, since initially, you perceive yourself as nothing but the body, your attention should focus on the breath and physical sensations, but never become an obsession with the body itself.

You are using the body as a springboard to dive into the self. Sthira sukha asana: be firm, be comfortable - that is your posture.

When you meditate or practice yoga, envision yourself as a monarch; you are a king, not a beggar. The one who excessively twists his body is like a beggar - have you ever seen a king do all that? Have you ever seen a king in a headstand? It would look absurd because he is a king, seated on his throne, mastering his universe. He doesn't need to engage in such nonsense.

That is the posture you need to assume - sit like a king, sit like a queen. Revel in the sensations of the body, experience its subtleties, and always maintain the mindset that "I am comfortable. There's no need to shift or change." Whatever posture is comfortable for you is acceptable, whether it's sitting on the floor, on a chair, or cross-legged. The specifics of the posture don't matter as much as the attitude and the intention behind it.

MUDRA

Where should you keep your hands? Place them wherever it's comfortable. There's a whole discipline in yoga dedicated to what you do with your hands -

the different types of mudras. But joining your thumb with your middle finger doesn't mean something magical will happen. You won't become enlightened just because your fingers are positioned a certain way. And not using a mudra doesn't mean you aren't meditating. Yes, you might see many enlightened people sitting with their fingers in what is recognized as a mudra, but often, that's just a natural position for them. Sometimes your fingers might be open, other times closed. Maybe you rest them on your lap - it doesn't matter. Your fingers are simply responding to what's happening inside you.

The posture of your hands should naturally reflect your inner state. You don't need to reverse engineer this by forcing your fingers into specific mudras. Let your hands be relaxed and natural. You don't have to practice all the different types of mudras. Focus on what's happening inside, and let your hands just be a part of that natural expression. You don't need to attach unnecessary meaning to those mudras - it's all deviation and distraction. Again, recognize the child inside you. The moment it sees, "Oh, I have hands, and I'm a yogi now. What can I do with my hands?" Please don't do anything. Stop being a child. You're a yogi. You're a ferocious lion. You are a king. You're not a child. Just keep your hands wherever they want to be as long as it's comfortable. That is why if you look at images of Shiva, he's sitting in a certain posture and his hands have assumed a certain Mudra. Shiva is usually depicted as holding his thumb and pointing fingers together. If you were to look at Buddha, he has both his hands on his lap. One on top of the other.

Now, what is the difference? Nothing. It is just our way of identifying. You can just as well paint a Buddha sitting in a yogic posture like Shiva, but that's not how you identify him. It helps you to identify him because you don't know how he looks. So certain remnants are what you're holding on to, the matted hair, the way he sits, the lotus posture, It is you who are obsessed with Buddha's lotus posture. Buddha was never obsessed with his lotus posture. In fact, Buddha never spoke about the lotus posture. He never spoke about asana. He only spoke about meditation. So is Patanjali. He's not talking about all the yogic postures. He's just saying sit comfortably. He says that perfection in an asana is achieved when the effort to perform it becomes effortless, and the infinite being within is reached. There, he's chopped the head of a so-called yogi - the one who's obsessed with yogasana.

Patanjali teaches that you cannot achieve perfection in an asana merely through physical effort. Instead, he says that an asana is perfected only when it becomes effortless - when it no longer feels like an effort at all.

This level of effortlessness aligns with enlightenment, suggesting that true mastery of an asana coincides with the perfection of your inner being.

According to Patanjali, striving in yoga isn't just about mastering physical postures; it's about reaching a state of effortlessness and realizing your infinite nature. In his view, any physical posture will inherently involve some discomfort due to the nature of the body, indicating that a perfectly comfortable asana doesn't exist. The real goal of yoga, therefore, is not to achieve a perfect posture but to attain a state of enlightenment where the physical discomforts are transcended, and your consciousness expands into its infinite potential. When this happens, the asana is said to reach its true completion.

When you look at statues of Buddha or Shiva, you see only their outer forms. Inside, they've reached the ultimate state. Their bodies have naturally assumed postures that accommodate the profound inner transformation they've experienced - the "internal explosion" of enlightenment that fills them with vastness. Initially, their bodies might have shifted or adjusted slightly, but ultimately, they settled into a posture that reflects deep internal comfort and stability.

As you venture deeper into yourself, your body will naturally find its most comfortable position. So, when beginning your practice, the key things to remember are firmness and comfort. Avoid getting caught up in the physical or mental gymnastics of perfecting your posture, and worrying about the position of your fingers, legs, or head. These details aren't as significant as what's happening inside you. What your meditation looks like from the outside isn't what's important; it's the internal experience and the transformations occurring within that truly matter.

PRANAYAMA - THE BREATH

So, once you have assumed a comfortable posture - a posture that allows you to move away from the body, from the experiences and sensations of the body to the object of your focus and awareness - you begin to take control over what's happening. Up until now, you have only acknowledged what has already happened. You always come last. A stimulus occurs, a thought process forms and that thought process initiates an action. Often, you arrive at the end of the action; sometimes, you arrive at the beginning.

What do I mean by "you come" or "you arrive?" It means becoming self-aware - those moments when you pause to see what you're doing. Once in a while, by mistake, accidentally, you happen to observe what's happening in your own life, your own thoughts, your own actions. You are permitted to watch only occasionally. Most of the time, you are pushed aside. You are not important. Your awareness and your consciousness are not important. The mind and body have conspired with each other and established their own kingdom, their own rules, and their own ways of doing things. You are outside the gates. Even to see what's happening, you have to take permission to get in. It is not easy. By mistake, if the door opens accidentally, you get a glimpse: "Oh, I can see a thought. I can recognize an emotion." That's about it.

That's why you're seeing things from very far away. You're not inside the gate; you're outside. That is life. You have been displaced from your center. You have been thrown out of your own kingdom. You are a king, but now only in name and form. All the affairs are being managed by the mind and the body. This is why the mind can drive you crazy - because it is not your kingdom; it is theirs. It is natural when you don't have a say in what's happening. Once in a while, you notice that something is going wrong. These "people" are breeding anger, pain, chaos, and confusion. There's too much drinking, too much smoking. It's your own mind and body, and only when these things flare up and begin to affect you do you actually notice them. That means it is not your kingdom. You are an outsider now. The body has become a slave to the mind. The mind has learned how to use the body because you don't have a say. That is why you can become overweight or develop unhealthy habits. That is why, when you decide to do something about it, it is not easy.

Exploring Unconsciousness

These are all signs that you are no longer the king. You can no longer just tell your mind, "Do this," or tell your body, "Do that." They'll respond with, "Who are you? Stand outside. Everything is automated here. Don't you dare come in and interfere with this process." They don't care whether they create anger or make you obese. What's important to them is that everything happens without any interference. That is what the mind wants. That is what the body wants. They want to follow their set patterns and don't care about the consequences. They'll do enough to keep you alive because they understand that if you're not alive, the game ends. Only in moments when your life is actually in danger do they stop what they're doing and come to your rescue. Other than that, they don't even care about you.

Yoga is the first time you want in. You want to enter those gates. You want to see what's happening there. You want to inspect the business and set things right because it has become clear that whatever is going on there is not what is supposed to be happening. There are too many things going on that shouldn't be. You can recognize it as the effects of life - too much anxiety, too much worry, a lot of unknowns, and uncertainty about your future. These are all signs that you're no longer at the center. You have been banished from your kingdom.

When did this happen? The first moment you became unconscious. That is what is recognized as birth. Birth is great unconsciousness. Nobody takes birth consciously. If you see a conscious baby, run - that's not a baby. Unconsciousness is what defines being an infant. You don't know how to read, how to write, or how to walk. You're learning all this. You don't know how to control your body. You don't even know who you are. If a child speaks as if they know life, and has an awareness of its purpose and meaning, be wary. The very definition of birth itself is an unconscious activity. So, there's no question of conscious birth. From then on, your life has just been happening. Once in a while, you watch it. You don't even interfere with the process. You just watch it.

Yoga is the greatest rebellion. It is a rebellion against the entire kingdom of your mind and body. It is a rebellion against the universe they have created for themselves. It is a rebellion against all the ideas and concepts, the understanding of life they have accepted as true. It is a rebellion against your own breath. It is a rebellion against everything you can recognize as you. That is why it is not an ordinary feat. That is why it takes tremendous courage to be a yogi, to call yourself a yogi.

If you truly understand yoga, it will be that moment when you decide: either you want to be a yogi, or you don't want to have anything to do with this: "I want to live in unconsciousness; I want to die in unconsciousness." Who's going to fight with the mind? Who's going to fight with the body? This is too much. It's going to be painful, sometimes brutal. The mind is going to be so vicious that it will attack you the moment you enter. It won't say, "Come, let me give you a tour of your inside." It sees you as the enemy. Why are you the enemy? Because you embody consciousness, aliveness, and truth - you are everything the mind is not. The mind is a lie, shrouded in darkness and operating automatically. It has spent years developing these habits and is heavily invested in maintaining its dream, reluctant to let go.

You, being who you are - the light, the source of everything - are the enemy of the mind. You have to accept this before entering. You are not welcome. Someone is there giving orders every single moment to throw you out. Every single thought in your mind has been instructed to not let you in. Each thought is like a soldier. The mind is the king. It has already given the order: "Don't let this conscious being in; he's going to ruin our business. Do you know what he's trying to do? He's trying to replace all of you with what he calls 'silence.' You will have no job. How many thoughts will disappear, will die, to accommodate this silence? And he's not going to stop with the elimination of one or two thoughts. He's going to keep on going because once he recognizes that you are the enemy, he has to eliminate you completely to become fully silent. And finally, he's going to come for me because this throne actually belongs to him. I tricked him. This idiot thinks birth is a great moment of consciousness. He does not understand that he was a king before he took birth. It is birth that made him a beggar. It is birth that attached him to a limited mind and body. Now, somehow, he's become aware of this knowledge. I don't know who gave him this knowledge, but I don't have any control over that. I can only control what's happening in my kingdom."

"He's gotten this knowledge from some other kingdom, from somewhere else. We have tried to eliminate this knowledge completely, but somewhere it remains. Now, he wants to know himself, and when he knows himself, he will know that he is the king. So what is my job? To make sure that he doesn't get in. Put as many soldiers as possible at the gate. Put all the forces at the entrance because that is where you can stop him easily. If he tries and fails, he'll go back. But if he succeeds a little, if he enters and manages to travel inward, then it will become harder and harder to stop him. He'll acquire the confidence that, yes, he can be in this realm. He can watch his thoughts. He can watch his actions. And then he will begin to feel comfortable. He'll begin to enjoy being here. Let us make sure that this doesn't happen." The moment you sit and close your eyes, know that the battle has started.

TRICK THE MIND

If you think going inward will be easy, you're in for a surprise. It is the hardest at the beginning. Your journey can never be harder than your early stages of trying to break through the wall that the mind has built for itself. Every thought will try to push you into action. There will be great exaggeration - exaggeration of pain, exaggeration of suffering. Your mind is going to scare you to the point where you think, "I don't want to see what's happening here. This is mayhem. And why are you reminding me of my childhood traumas? I thought I had forgotten all that. Why are you taking me back to childhood?" That is how the mind can throw you out. It's trying to scare you.

So what is your tool? What is your weapon to go inward? You can't go in naked; you will be slashed to pieces. You have to be smart. You have to trick the mind. There is no other way to enter other than by tricking the mind. You have to make the mind feel that you are only there as a brief visitor. You're not going to stay there forever. You have to limit the duration of your inward entry. That's going to be the first indication to the mind that, okay, he's going to do this exercise for maybe an hour. After that, he's going to get up and go away. Still, it won't allow you to do it comfortably, but at least you've gotten the first instruction in: it's momentary. I'm not going to be here forever.

Approach your inward journey systematically. One of the simplest ways to introduce a system is by keeping your practice time-bound. This will do two things. First, it will help the mind relax a bit. Second, it will ensure that at least for that duration, you don't give up. If you say, "I want to be on the inside for the next hour," you at least know when not to quit. Otherwise, because it's so challenging, so hard, and because you're constantly being pushed out, it is very easy to give up. So, time helps.

Apart from that, you are carrying your intellectual understanding. These are some tools that you're carrying. When a thought approaches you, at least you have a counterargument. When it brings a spear, at least you have another spear to counter it. That is what an argument is at the end of the day. If a thought wins, you're dead: Out. If you win, you continue further. It's as simple as that. All that knowledge, all that wisdom you've acquired during the preparatory phase of yoga will help you counter your thoughts.

And then, you need to befriend the body. This is a very important step. You are fighting against the mind. The mind is immediate, impulsive, and constantly trying to push you out. But there is the body, which takes time to recognize the enemy. The body is not immediate. The body does not care whether you watch it or not because it is slow. It is only after a while - sometimes weeks, even months - that it understands that it is being watched, and by then, the watching itself has become a process, so there is no resistance. That is why you can watch the body without being pushed out. It is always the mind that is trying to throw you out, not your body.

That's where Patanjali introduces a beautiful, elegant, time-hardened, and proven way of entering: your inner world: pranayama, or breath control. By using the breath as your friend, as your ally, you can counter the arguments of the mind and gain entry into your inner world. Pranayama is the regulation of breath and the restraint of mental activity that results in the ability to concentrate and direct the mind. Patanjali is directly saying that your breath is going to help you direct, control, and understand the mind.

Literally, he's saying to befriend the body because breath belongs to the body - it has nothing to do with the mind. With breath on your side, there is a disguise. Now the mind is confused. You're not bringing your light of awareness directly to shine on its activities; you are only using that light to illuminate parts of the body. You're illuminating the breath. So the mind is opposed to light, but it is not too concerned because you are investigating the body, not the mind. Even then, you can hear the mind screaming. You can hear the conversations. You can hear the resistance. But that is nothing compared to entering straight and deciding to watch your thoughts.

The purpose of going in is to watch your thoughts and understand what's happening. Watching thoughts will be a constant, eternal process of yoga. Yet, Patanjali doesn't introduce you to that practice directly. He tells you to focus on something else: the breath. Why? Because he knows and understands that it is next to impossible to watch the mind directly. The mind is so tricky, so cunning, that it will put you to sleep and start drifting in thoughts. Instead of watching thoughts, you end up watching the activities of thoughts. Instead of watching your mind, you become a part of the mind.

The mind knows only one way of dealing with consciousness: by making you unconscious. That is why you struggle. Meditation is a struggle because you are consciousness, you are awareness. You're trying to watch what's happening, but your mind is unconsciousness. It immediately takes all your desires in that moment - the desire to meditate, the desire to be watchful, the desire to be silent - and turns them into concepts, putting you into an unconscious state. That is why you either fall asleep or the disturbance becomes so overwhelming that you cannot sit and watch your thoughts. It becomes so scary that you give up. You would rather do something else. It is easier to sit and watch a movie than to sit and watch your thoughts. Why? Because there is resistance there.

Pranayama is the trick. It is a method, a device through which you can trick the mind. When Patanjali talks about directing the mind, in a way, he's saying trick the mind. Now, let's understand what pranayama is not. Just like the physical postures of yoga that have become their own discipline and deviated completely from the true purpose of yoga - moving towards self-realization - pranayama has also become a separate discipline of breathing exercises. Instead of using the breath to control the mind, you are using the breath to control yourself. You have become so obsessed with altering the breath, holding the breath, and changing the rhythm of the breath that you have confused the actual purpose of Pranayama. Instead of helping you to control the mind, the practice has become so dominant that it is controlling you.

There is a subtle but very significant difference between pranayama as an exercise and pranayama as a discipline. As an exercise, it is totally useless. Yes, you might win a few accolades or even an award if you can hold your breath for ten minutes, but it won't help you in your yogic journey. If controlling the breath is your purpose, then you don't need to study the scriptures, understand meditation, or prepare yourself for the battle. Just keep altering your breath. Keep pushing your breath. Every day, in every session, hold your breath longer, take deeper breaths, exhale deeply, inhale deeply. Your breath changes, so you develop the ability to take in more breath, take in more oxygen, and you can boast about that. You might say, "I can take in twice as much oxygen as you can." But that doesn't prove you're any more intelligent or advanced in your spiritual journey.

Pranayama is not about breathing exercises. Many meditation schools and spiritual schools practice pranayama like dumbbell exercises, physically doing something when pranayama is actually about watching the breath. Pranayama is bringing your awareness to the breath so that you are not thrown out by the mind. The breath is right at the door; it is between the outside and the inside. This is where you have to be the most careful because that is where all the guards are. All your thoughts are stacked up against you. Remember, you are an intruder.

Now you can watch this. If you are careful enough, you will see there is someone going in and out. Although this kingdom is closed and nobody comes out or goes in, there is this one guy allowed free entry: the breath. There is your opening. It's not impossible to break through this wall. Without the breath, you would not even know where to begin. You'd be trying to scale the walls, trying to break the wall. Unless you have enormous strength, enormous willpower, and are willing to go through that frustrating journey for months and years, you will easily give up. But if you're smart, if you have read your scriptures, if you have intellectually understood the nature of the mind and the body, you will see that the breath is allowed inside. The breath has access to the realms of the mind and the body. It is coming from outside and also going back out.

Now, if you can somehow hitch a ride on the breath, it is possible that you will be allowed in. That is what Pranayama is. Pranayama is not trying to wrestle with the breath, not to overpower it, not to increase its ability to go inward and outward. It is just to use it, just to hitch a ride and go in. That happens when you sit and watch your breath. The regulation of breath and the restraint of mental activity result in the ability to concentrate and direct the mind. The regulation of breath is nothing but watching the breath. Watching the breath is what will lead to the restraint of mental activity. When you are watching your breath, the noise of the mind reduces, the chaos of the mind reduces, and the disturbance reduces.

Because the mind cannot reject the breath, it becomes your eternal companion. As you travel with the breath, the mind, grudgingly, has to accommodate you. You can go as far as the breath goes. However, there is a limitation to the breath. It cannot access the inner realms of the mind, but at least it provides an entry point. You can see things more clearly when you're on the inside. Your entire life you have tried to understand what's happening on the inside by looking from somewhere far away. Now, you've been given access to the inside. You have tricked the mind and entered in.

If that entry has happened, if you are able to stay in for a little longer, and then if you are able to let go of your attachment to the breath, Pranayama is complete. Pranayama has served its purpose.

When does Pranayama become a mere breathing exercise? When you start boasting about your accomplishments. The more things you do with your breath, the less you are moving inward. You should do as little as possible. There is no need to interfere with the breath. However, sometimes when you are unable to watch the breath, you can regulate it, but only to help you relax.

For example, you begin to notice that you're falling asleep. How can you stay awake? The moment you watch the breath, because it is so subtle and you're not used to watching something so subtle, you may fall asleep. That is when you breathe consciously. You inhale consciously, you exhale consciously. When you do that, it is natural for the rhythm of the breath to alter a bit. You might take a deeper breath, you might exhale deeply, you might hold the breath a little longer. It is perfectly fine as long as you're not using that as a tool to control the breath. As long as you're using it as a tool to control the mind, to stay awake, to stay alert, then it's fine. That much interference with the breath is allowed.

That is why it is called Pranayama. Prana is breath, which is life force itself, and yama is exercise. It does allow you to interfere with it, but not more than necessary. Why is Pranayama so important? It is so crucial that Buddha prescribed it as the only method to awakening. He said simply, "Watch your breath." The breath will get you in. Once you get in, keep following the same trajectory of the breath even when there is no breath. You will connect with silence. You will connect with stillness. And then you will eventually become enlightened. It's the same rhythm of breath that you're holding on to. Even when the breath is no longer there, your practice has become strong enough to simulate silence. And once you can artificially imagine silence, it's only a matter of time before you actually connect with it. So for Buddha, watching the breath was the entire method.

Pranayama and vipassana are not two different things. The only difference is that in yoga, pranayama is used as a tool to gain entry, and then you drop it. In vipassana, you hold on to it. However, you do not manipulate it or interfere with the process but explore the subtler and subtlest realms of the breath. Pranayama is important because it introduces you to the infinite capabilities of your true self. Your mind and body are set. They follow a pattern. They know when to sleep, when to wake up, how much to eat, and what to do. All these processes are automatic, built-in, but you can alter them. Pranayama is the first indication that it is actually possible to change this automated process of the mind and the body. You can see that with your own breath because the breath is the first thing you control on the inward journey.

By your own will, by your own conscious choice, you can pause a breath - a breath that has been automatic for years, for decades. By your conscious will, you can stop it. Of course, the conditioning kicks in, and you cannot hold the breath too long. You have to give up. But at least every time you control it, it indicates that it's actually possible because breath is one of the most automated processes. It is the least conscious part of your being. You're conscious of your actions. You're conscious of your thoughts sometimes. But how often do you sit and watch the breath? It belongs to the unconscious. It belongs to the automatic. And anything that belongs to the automatic also belongs to the mind. By watching the breath, you will begin to realize that it is actually possible to push the boundaries of the mind and the body. You will begin to realize that you can stay awake longer than your mind and body currently allow you to.

The first day I sat in meditation, I spent half the time asleep. Then, after a month, I was aware when I fell asleep, and it only lasted maybe ten or twenty minutes. What does that mean? It means that by consciously watching my breath, I altered the automatic process of sleep. Sleep is deep unconsciousness. So, watching the breath is how you learn that it is possible to gain control over your mind. If you try to control the mind directly, you will lose. You need a trick. You need a method. And pranayama is that trick.

WITHDRAWAL OF SENSES

There are a few more important sutras that Patanjali gives to help us understand pranayama. Pranayama is also a way of controlling your senses, what he calls the withdrawal of senses, to help awaken something inside. When your senses are withdrawn, when one part of you shuts down - the imaginary part of you, the sensory part of you - the silent part of you awakens. You can start seeing things differently for the first time. This seeing is very different from seeing through your senses. Through your senses, all your experiences are divided and limited. They are chopped up into innumerable pieces. At most, you can understand one piece at a time. By their very nature, senses are divided, and that is why they can so effectively draw your attention away from the non-divided. When something gets divided, your attention has to be dispersed between those parts.

The movement from one thing to another, from seeing to hearing, from hearing to smelling, and within each sense, the divisions - sometimes you see clearly, sometimes you see far, and at other times you see things that are close by - all this provides enough engagement and entertainment for your mind to be occupied. That game in totality is what we identify as life experiences.

If yoga is about realizing something that is eternally there, something that can never be divided, something seamless, then the only way to realize the limitless, the eternal - the silent - is to withdraw from the chopped-up world of senses. The withdrawal of the senses from their external objects and focusing them internally on the breath is Pranayama. Patanjali is saying that Pranayama, the practice itself, is a way of withdrawing yourself from the world of external senses and objects.

Understanding your senses and the control they have over your life is the starting point of withdrawal. Without understanding, it's easy to conclude that your senses are working in your favor, helping you to experience things. At a certain level, this is true. You cannot see without your eyes. You cannot smell without your nose. You cannot taste without your mouth. You know where your senses are and the general territory where maximum sense perception is happening. But are they really helping you to experience life or are they actually blocking your pure perception of life?

That's the deeper philosophical question. Have you simply assumed that your senses are illuminating things when, in fact, they are actually blocking them? What if, for every object your senses illuminate, they hide a million others? What if, for every sound you can hear, there are a million others you cannot? How would you know this, because this is your only experience of sense perception.

You've not had any opportunity to compare your senses with a higher sense because you are the highest form of sensory organism. You regard your senses to be more superior than those of other creatures because your senses provide you with the best possible collective experience of life that you recognize as life. That is why you would not want to trade your senses with any other animal's senses. Yes, dogs can smell perhaps a hundred times better than you, but you would not want a dog's sense of smell. It is useless in your world. More than useless, it might even be a nuisance. Why would you need to smell a hundred times better? Because your world is more visual and auditory, there is no necessity to smell everything. Imagine what a formal handshake would be in a world where you could smell a hundred times more. It wouldn't be a handshake; it would be sniffing, like the way dogs greet each other. We know how dogs greet each other. Let's not go into the details.

Senses are not superior or inferior. They are perfectly aligned with the experiences you are having. In your world, your senses are perfect. You cannot even imagine anything better. If you already have good eyesight, there is no need to enhance it. Enhancing your eyesight will not help because you can only see those things that you are conditioned to see. If you were suddenly given a special kind of eyesight where you could see more colors or see farther, you couldn't even conceptualize what that would feel like. It is impossible to see something other than what you are conditioned to see.

So, in a way, the world isn't simply sitting there for your senses to perceive; your world is being created along with the process of perception. Literally, your world is nothing but an extension of your senses. This is why you cannot conclusively say that your senses are helping you. It is like saying, "My senses are useful because they are helping me to see the world." Well, they have created the world. If they have created the world, then to say that they are helping you to see the world is pointless.

For all you know, this whole world of experiences - all your sensory perceptions put together - might actually be blocking your true experience of life. As Lao Tzu says, "Colors can blind your eyes. Sounds can deafen your ears." How can this be? When my senses are opening up my world, helping me to see more and hear more, how is it possible that they are actually crippling me?

It is possible because you have no way of comparing the absolute reality with your reality. The only reality you are familiar with is your reality, and that is why you call it reality. If you were to compare your world of senses to a heightened state of awareness, an awakened state, a Buddha state, you would immediately see that this world is not real. It's a world of illusions, a world of mirages, a world of lights and shadows, a world of movement and stillness. There's nothing real here. You call it real because this is the only thing you know.

That is why you are trying to break through the veil of thoughts. That is why you are trying to meditate. That is why you want to be a yogi. You want to break through this illusion. Why else would you strive to awaken if you were not asleep? So you have to assume that if you are striving for awakening, it means you are asleep right now. Now, if you are asleep, why do you feel like you are awake? What is giving you this perception of wakefulness? It's your senses. Because you are able to see, you conclude that you must be awake, without realizing the process of seeing itself might be blinding to your pure self.

It's just like a prism. When sunlight passes through a prism, it breaks up into multiple colors. You might look at those colors and say, "This prism is actually illuminating the world of colors. It's helping me see all the different qualities of light." But in reality, it is blocking the pure light. It is restricting it, squeezing it. In that squeezing, in that restriction, pure light splits up. Color is impurity when compared to pure light. Pure light has no color, which is why it can illuminate all things. If light itself had some color, it would not be nearly as useful as it is now. Because light has no color, it can illuminate everything.

So what is the prism doing? It is blocking something pure and dividing it into parts. And as curious, inquisitive children who enjoy playing with things, we look at this as illumination. We think, "My senses are helping me see the world." But in fact, they have divided you and your experiences completely. That is why you are always in a state of unrest in the world of senses. Even if all your sensual desires are fulfilled, you will still feel incomplete. The senses themselves are blocking something that is already complete. How can they complete completeness? You are already complete. You are pure consciousness, pure being, and that is what you're striving for. There is something within you, a space, a zone where you can be fully contented, fully blissful, above and beyond all pain and suffering. Isn't that what you're searching for in life? A moment of pure ecstasy, a moment of pure joy that is not attached to anything, that is your own. You can experience it whenever you want, as many times as you want, but in the world of senses, your happiness, your joy, is always limited and connected to something. You are never free to enjoy your sense pleasures as much as you want, whenever you want. By their very nature, they are incomplete and divided.

Withdrawing yourself from the senses, while it may appear to be life-negative, is the only life-positive thing that you can do. When you're able to withdraw yourself from the senses, you're also withdrawing yourself from sleep. By the very nature of things, if you withdraw yourself from the world of sleep, you have to sooner or later wake up. There is no choice. You cannot say, "I don't want to sleep, but at the same time, I don't want to wake up." If you decide not to sleep, then you are choosing to wake up.

The withdrawal of the senses from their external objects and focusing them internally on the breath is pranayama. Now, what is this withdrawing? How do you withdraw? Withdrawal is not shutting down your senses because there's really no way to shut them down. If you decide, "Okay, I don't want to see," pick one sense, the visual sense, and say, "I want to withdraw from the world of visual senses." So, how do you do it? I'll close my eyes. It's so simple. Okay, close your eyes. Have you actually withdrawn from the world of seeing? Not at all. You are still continuing to see. Either you're seeing the darkness, the back of your eyelids, which is still seeing, or you are imagining things, which means you're continuing to see. Your world of senses has not stopped just because you've closed your eyes.

Withdrawal is a process. Withdrawal is a journey. In fact, that is the entire journey of yoga. Ultimately, when you're able to fully withdraw from the world of senses, you will awaken fully. The moment you understand that there's no immediate quick shortcut for withdrawing from the senses, you will approach it differently. We can see this in the world of our experiences: There is an exception to every rule we have set for our senses and what they are capable of. Even with what the mind and body are capable of, you draw the limitation. You say, "This is what the body can do; this is what it cannot do." And if you search hard enough, you will find an exception to that rule. At least there will be one exception that will break that rule.

You draw a conclusion that human beings possess a certain kind of intelligence, that this is what they are capable of. You draw the boundaries based on your investigation, your understanding of the brain, the mind, and the body. Then if you search for intelligence that is higher, deeper, and greater than that, you will find it. Draw your rules of physical strength, and you will find someone somewhere capable of breaking those rules. The whole of human history is filled with experiences of extraordinary sense perceptions, individuals who have done something extraordinary with their senses, knowingly or unknowingly. For example, people who talk about the afterlife or near-death experiences claim to have traveled to the other side, where their body is dead, their eyes and ears are useless, their brain is damaged. And still, they are seeing, hearing, and experiencing life with more intensity using a body that is on the verge of death.

Now, that is an exception that makes us question the nature of the senses. If senses are the only tools I have for perceiving the world, then why am I finding these exceptions? How is it possible that when it seems like the body should have no capabilities of perceiving - physically, you can see it is damaged beyond repair - yet, when this person comes back, when the body revives, they talk about their experiences as if they had all their sensory perceptions intact and something more?

NO SLEEP

These exceptions are clues for us to understand that there is something above and beyond the world of our senses. One particular example comes to mind. There was a man named Nguyen Van Thai who lived in a small village in Vietnam. He was famous for his ability to stay awake, to not sleep. It is said that he had not slept a wink in sixty years. People were amazed. First, they wanted to understand if this was true. With a little bit of investigation, they figured out that he was not lying. He actually did not sleep. He knew nothing about sleep and did not even have a desire to sleep. He was awake throughout the day and night and had been in that state for the last sixty years.

He was perfectly healthy. He did not get tired unnecessarily, and he did not have any ailments resulting from this lack of sleep. Researchers were baffled. They wanted to understand what was going on. Was it hormonal or biological? They tried to figure out how he could stay awake because we know how important sleep is. People can die if they don't get enough sleep. How is it that this man has transcended sleep?

They conducted all kinds of experiments to try and figure out the root cause of this, but they could not find any. They could not identify a single neurological, biological, or hormonal process contributing to this unique ability of his. People then started regarding him as a saint, calling him the "wakeful saint." They believed he had been given special powers that made him unique and special, leading them to worship him.

In Buddhism, there is only one other individual credited with the ability to stay awake for an extended period - Buddha, who stayed awake for forty years. He was an enlightened, awakened, liberated soul. For us, wakefulness and spiritual awakening are synonymous. If you are not spiritually awakened, if something special has not happened to you, then you are like the rest of us. So, if you can stay awake without falling asleep, people might even believe you are not mortal.

With Nguyen, there's something else happening. Now, what is the secret? It turns out the secret was something else altogether. Yes, he practiced a bit of meditation and was spiritual, but the true secret lay in a combination of activities and the environment he was in, which created unique conditions for him to stay awake. Interestingly, he was unaware that these conditions had removed the necessity for sleep. He did not consciously try to stay awake.

Firstly, he lived in a very small village amidst nature and was a survivor of the Vietnam War. His sleeplessness began because he was so traumatized during the war that he couldn't sleep at night - a case of what we now call PTSD (post-traumatic stress disorder). However, unlike many others with PTSD, who eventually return to normal sleep patterns, he never did.

During the war, he moved into a small hut that he built for himself in the middle of the forest, and that is where he lived. His lifestyle was extraordinarily simple. He lived in that hut, did a bit of farming, and kept to himself. When a reporter visited him to try and understand more about this sleepless man, he discovered something unique. There was another house apart from where he was living, where Nguyen spent his nights. During the day, he was in his small hut farming and doing simple activities, but during the night, he stayed in this other house. The reporter found this curious and thought that maybe the secret to Nguyen's sleeplessness was in this house. Perhaps he was doing something there that kept him awake.

They figured out that he spent the entire night sitting and preparing rice wine. That was his work. All night, he cooked the rice or followed whatever process was involved in converting rice to wine. He drank this strong local liquor almost all the time, and it was more than just a drink; it was his main source of sustenance, even more than actual food. That's when all the pieces started falling into place. It was the rice wine that was keeping him awake and his desire to prepare the wine that motivated him to stay awake. He didn't even think about all these things consciously because he was so poor. He couldn't afford to prepare the rice wine during the day because he had to farm and do other activities to sustain his life. He figured out that night was the best time to prepare the wine. Because he had done this repeatedly, eventually, there was no need or necessity for him to sleep.

Now, what this man's life tells us is that we have hardly scratched the surface of understanding what our senses are and what they are capable of doing. The biggest limitation the senses have imposed on us is a limited understanding of our minds and bodies because we look at ourselves through our senses. Everything you know about your mind and body comes from your senses, from watching others, and from observing experiences on the outside and sometimes on the inside, but it's all filtered through a prism. So, everything you know about yourself is actually a tiny subset of what you truly are.

In examples like this, we see what happens when certain conditions come together where that prism is removed or shifted, allowing the pure light to pass through. Even if we find a single exception, it invalidates the general theory of what we know about the mind and the body. Because what is truth? Truth is something that is true with no exceptions.

The sun could be shining continuously for a thousand years. But if, for whatever reason, it decides not to shine for a single moment, if it withdraws its light for just one moment, what would that tell us? It would tell us that we know nothing about the sun. Everything we thought we knew about the sun would be wrong. It is these exceptions that illuminate the secrets of life, not the general rules. General rules exist because we have created them based on our observations and understanding. It's only when the light breaks through the cloud and we see something different that our attention is caught and we are prompted to investigate further.

A man who has not slept for sixty years is telling us something entirely different about the mind and the body. He's saying that human beings are creatures of conditioning. It is possible to decondition ourselves. It is possible to change our minds and bodies. It is possible to transcend the limitations of the mind and body by altering the conditions that have restricted them. Sometimes it happens accidentally, as in the case of Nguyen Van Thai. But in your case, because it has not happened accidentally, you don't see that it is possible.

We have examples of individuals who have consciously found a way to break through the limitations of their senses, and that is what yoga is. Why is a yogi almost regarded as a superhuman? Why do we revere him? Why do we regard him as the highest expression of life? Why haven't we forgotten the Buddha? Why is it impossible to forget him? Because he has done something to alter the conditioning of his life consciously. Through that process, he has shown us that we are nothing but creatures of conditioning. It is all linked to our senses.

If, accidentally, your senses are withdrawn, as in the case of Nguyen Van Thai, where the rice wine dulled his senses and the desire to prepare that rice wine kept him awake, a condition of watchfulness and sleep was created unconsciously. The wine induced a state of relaxation and numbness, eliminating the need for separate sleep. This combination of conditions kept him relaxed and awake simultaneously. People often consume alcohol to relax and numb their senses, and in his case, the process of preparing wine added the condition of wakefulness. In a way, he was meditating without knowing anything about meditation.

Literally, what is meditation? What is yoga? It is the merging of wakefulness and sleep. If you can be perfectly asleep inside and perfectly watch that sleep, then you are above and beyond your senses. You have withdrawn your senses. This happened to him unknowingly, but for the Buddha, it happened consciously. He strived for it, created the conditions, and eventually, it happened.

The process is the same; what is needed is a deeper understanding of the world of senses and the process of withdrawal. Regulation of inhalation, exhalation, and the suspension of breath are all part of this. The first step is the identification of the senses and understanding that they are not illuminating anything; they are actually blocking something. We are only seeing through a prism, through a keyhole. Yoga aims to break down the wall that blocks us from pure perception of life so that we can see without our eyes, hear without our ears, smell without our nose, touch without our body, and be alive without anything blocking that perception of aliveness.

As of now, you're alive, but your aliveness is confined to the body, illuminated by your senses. You consider this - your body, your mind - as your most precious possession. Yet, in the pursuit of understanding the nature of reality, these are not just unhelpful; they are obstacles. They serve purposes in the world, but for those seeking awakening, they are not merely useless - they represent the limitations that must be transcended.

Regulating inhalation, exhalation, and breath suspension are methods to withdraw from the senses. Watching the breath helps control your senses, diminishing their influence and impact. You can manipulate the breath - inhale deeply, exhale fully, even pause it temporarily. This manipulation is vital as long as it serves to divert your focus from the traditional operations of your five primary senses, enabling you not to engage in the usual sensory-driven creation of your world.

When you sit in meditation with your eyes closed, you aim not to perceive anything externally; you're striving to turn inward. You create stories internally, continuing to talk to yourself. Instead of acting externally, you're engaging internally. "Oh, now I'm meditating. I'm learning how to relax." And thus, the internal conversation begins, mirroring the external world. It is through language and this internal dialogue that you've constructed the world outside. The world makes no sense if you can't talk about it, much like the internal world created by your dialogue, which crafts a familiar illusion that keeps you stuck in the world of illusion.

This is why Patanjali suggests using your breath as a means to distract and withdraw from the senses. Your breath becomes the initial focus - the starting point for what comes next: concentration. You cannot concentrate while lost in your senses. You must either focus or remain lost. Pranayama, then, is the transitional phase between being lost in sensory perception and focusing internally, which will eventually broaden and become your ultimate reality.

Breath control in this context is not merely an exercise, a destination, or a standalone technique. It is a crucial tool for your inward journey.

PRATYAHARA - SENSE CONTROL

Pratyahara, or sense control, is a vital yet immensely challenging aspect of yoga. It's the limb where you heighten your awareness, sharpening your ability to distinguish between yourself and your experiences. Here, you draw a line between the silence and the noise, between stillness and movement, grasping what truly belongs to you while releasing what does not. Pratyahara is derived from two Sanskrit words: "praty," meaning against, and "ahara," meaning food. Essentially, it's an ancient, elegant way of saying "diet" - not just in terms of what you eat, but more so in how you feed your senses. It's about not overindulging, not out of restriction but out of a choice to focus on what nourishes you truly and deeply.

Pratyahara is not inherently negative, unlike the concept of dieting, which often carries a negative connotation for those who love food. Dieting suggests a restriction, a conscious choice to reduce intake, and it's about permanent sacrifice - you can't defer today's skipped breakfast to tomorrow.

However, pratyahara involves a more profound element of choice and awareness. It's not just about pushing away or cutting out; it's about consciously choosing what to engage with and what to withdraw from, based on what nourishes and sustains your deeper self. In this sense, pratyahara is about reducing sensory overload to better connect with the inner essence, rather than a permanent denial of experiences.

Pratyahara is profoundly different. In the internal realm, controlling your senses and moving away from sensory pleasures only distances you from them momentarily. Beyond this lies an entire ocean of limitless pleasure. What might appear negative is actually propelling you toward the infinite. That sacrifice you make - pushing away a thought, detaching from your senses, and from people and experiences - might seem negative, both to an outside observer and to you, initially, because you haven't yet arrived at that vast ocean. But with time, you'll realize that there are no true sacrifices on the spiritual path. If we use the word 'sacrifice,' it's about trading lesser pleasures for greater ones, lesser attachments for the ultimate connection to your true self, and illusion for reality.

There's not even a comparison. That's why one day, you will laugh - laugh at how little was asked of you and yet how reluctant you were to let go. Like a child, you clung to your world of ideas, your imaginations, your senses, because you knew nothing else. That was your life, so naturally, you clung to it. But understanding is what frees you from this attachment to your senses. Now, how do we know this for sure?

"I am willing to work on detaching myself from the senses. I'm going to do something very few people have done - at least nobody in my family has. They don't know anything about pratyahara. None of my friends do this, and nobody I know in my real world is doing this. They aren't trying to control their senses. At every opportunity, they plan vacations to fill their senses with new experiences, more experiences. In fact, that is their life. I want more. I'm not satisfied with who I am. I want to travel more, do more, see more, eat more."

Now here, I am saying, "I want to withdraw from the world of senses." They wouldn't understand what that means. Now, I have to fight against all of them to hold on to this idea. That is why, in a way, you have to fight to just go and sit quietly because your friends and family members aren't just outside; they're inside your head. They are you. They are your voice. So, they will continue to try and convince you that you're wasting your time, wasting your life. While you sit still doing nothing for an hour, they'll say, "Look what we did. Look what we created: memories, experiences. What memories did you collect? You wasted an hour of your life. We took twenty pictures in one hour - pictures that we can go back to and remember those moments. What do you have to remember?" There's a contradiction.

The whole world of experiences, what people are doing, what people are thinking about, is the exact opposite of pratyahara. Now, if you have to convince yourself to do this, you must be sure about the reward. At least intellectually, you should have understood that there is a reward, a greater reward. Otherwise, there's no way you can maintain that practice. It is in the very nature of things. You are moving toward enlightenment because enlightenment exists, and it is an experience that completes you. It is the best of all experiences. It is the ultimate experience. Imagine if this experience were not as exciting, as exhilarating, as it is portrayed. There's no way you would put in all that effort. You would ask, "For what?" Somewhere deep inside, you know that enlightenment is an experience worth having. "That is why I'm willing to be a yogi - the one who battles his senses." Literally, that is the definition of a yogi.

Apart from the meaning of the word that implies bringing everything together, a yogi is also a fighter. The very word connotes fighting against your own mind, against your own senses. You are willing to do this because you understand that there is an ultimate experience waiting for you. But where is the proof? Of course, I know that unless I experience it myself, I will not truly know what it feels like. But are there any signs in our scriptures? Are there any indications of the nature of enlightenment? Or in my own life, have I accidentally fallen into that state, allowing me to at least say that it has happened to me accidentally, and now I want to move towards it consciously? The answer is yes. Not only are the remnants of that experience dispersed in almost all spiritual scriptures - if you know how to read them - but also an understanding of the ultimate experience, and what it feels like, can be found. We find words and descriptions in scriptures that give us a sense of what a deeper dive into our inner being feels like. Not just in the scriptures, but you have internal experiences too. You know what bliss is, and you understand what deeper states of relaxation are.

SEEK INTOXICATION

There one word you need to search for: intoxication. Hold on to that word - it is your raft. You're not seeking momentary, fleeting happiness. You're not searching for God, Jesus, Buddha, or deeper meaning. None of those things. You are searching for intoxication. You want to be so completely intoxicated that you forget the mind and body entirely and become the intoxication itself. Only complete intoxication can fulfill. More drink is the only thing that can further intoxicate a drunkard. There is no other way. If he has figured out that drinking leads to intoxication, then he's found his method. Continue drinking, and you'll be intoxicated to the point where you might even leave this realm. However, the problem is that all intoxicants in the world create dependency and attachment - you're not truly free. Once the intoxication wears off, you fall hard. With the same intensity that you elevated yourself to those higher realms, you will crash back down.

Intoxication is real. It is a part of our spiritual language, a part of our human culture. For example, the Greeks worshiped a fertility symbol called Bacchus, originally from the Thracians, from whom the Greeks borrowed this symbolism. The Thracians were very primitive - not in a negative sense, but in that they were simple, rooted, and down-to-earth. As farmers, the crops they produced and the food they created were their life. Naturally, they worshiped what their farming yielded. So, they created a symbolic representation of all the bounty of farming and identified it as Bacchus, the fertility god. Then, when they discovered wine and its intoxicating properties, derived from the same crops they grew, their appreciation and love for this fertility symbol reached its pinnacle. From being just a sustainer of life, it became the ultimate destination because they could see nothing more divine than intoxication. Anyone whose mind has not been polluted with false ideas of intoxication will have no trouble accepting that intoxication is a divine quality.

How else can you forget the pain of your mind and body? What is awakening, what is enlightenment, if not total intoxication? Bacchus became a symbol of ultimate pleasure, of wine, drinking, and partying. Eventually, when the Greeks adopted him, they embraced the most superficial understanding that he represented pleasure. That is why Bacchus is depicted as a young adult, his hair replaced with grapevines, and vines girdling him - a literal human personification of nature. Nature herself is intoxicated, possessing all the ingredients necessary to intoxicate us. It only took some time for humans to discover this. Once they learned how to make beer from grain and wine from grapes, they had found their god. There was no need to search for anything beyond.

Of course, the Greeks embraced merely the idea of external pleasure, to the extent that one pope even wanted a statue of Bacchus in the church. Here was a holy man, dedicated to the service of God and renouncing all life's pleasures, yet he ordered the inclusion of the god of wine, dance, and the ultimate symbol of sensory pleasure. This epitomizes perfect hypocrisy: preaching to the world to abstain from sex and pleasure, dedicating oneself to the service of God, while secretly worshiping pleasure. This highlights the dichotomy within humanity. There's a part of us that inherently understands what intoxication is - you cannot strip this from a human. In one way or another, everyone knows what it is to forget the body, whether through sex, moments of immense joy and wonder, or through intoxication, and there are several ways to achieve this, albeit momentarily.

Yet, religions have historically condemned these paths to intoxication. They have attempted to steer humanity away from all intoxicants, replacing the true intoxication of the divine with a contrived, conceptual, imaginary intoxication of heaven and hell. Essentially, they urge people to forsake the real, tangible fruits that can truly intoxicate, for plastic fruits - ideas of heaven and hell, redemption, and sacrifice - which can never lead to real intoxication but only to more suffering and confusion. You are left with nothing but the act of sacrifice itself, receiving in return nothing but a promise, an idea.

On the other hand, existentially, there is a process through which you sacrifice the momentary pleasures of life, the fleeting sensory pleasures, to experience a limitless drunkenness. One such system, one such process, is yoga. Yoga is about withdrawing yourself from the world of limited senses, where all your experiences are divided, to a realm where everything is connected, where a single drop can keep you intoxicated for eternity. There is such a wine, and you are that winemaking machine. If only you know how to find that sweet spot from where the nectar is dripping. You know the machine is there. You know the mechanism is there. You hear the sounds. That's what life is. You run around it, worship it, sometimes hug that machine, lick it, do whatever you want to it. You fall at its feet, but you don't realize that you need to drink from that machine. You need to find where the nectar is dripping from. You can hear the sounds, and that is what drives you crazy because you are not far away.

There is a constant reminder that what is missing is simply a deeper experience - a deeper understanding of yourself that can help you taste that wine. You cannot rest without tasting it, because that intoxication is your completion; that is your true nature. When your mind and body are erased, that is when you will know the actual meaning of being drunk. The drunkenness that you know of is nothing compared to the divine drunkenness. What we are searching for are those grapes that yield that wine, which we can use to create the ultimate intoxicant. One drop of that nectar, one drop of that elixir of life, and you are transformed forever. Yes, you can recognize your mind, you can recognize your body, you can still play the games of life, but you're drunk. You're complete from the inside.

The way to that divine drunkenness, the method, is withdrawal. This is what Pratyahara signifies - dieting for your senses. As long as you are attached to the limited senses, you will not search for the ultimate. Your senses are limited because the world of experiences you receive through your senses are merely names and labels compared to the real intoxicant that resides within. They all carry the label "wine." You read it, you understand it, but the experience is missing. That is why your senses can never introduce you to your awakened state. They cannot reveal the true nature of your being, nor can they guide you to that ocean of intoxication. They are just names, just ideas. At most, they can point to it; they can serve as signposts, but you cannot grasp drunkenness through them. You cannot see, hear, smell, taste, or touch drunkenness. Drunkenness is an internal quality.

You know what drunkenness is - when you see less, hear less, feel less, when all your senses are reeling under the influence of an intoxicant. When your senses are dulled and your awareness is shifted to a different realm, your attention directed elsewhere, that is the essence of intoxication. We see this, even in a limited way, when observing a drunk person. A drunken man is consumed by his own experience. But, of course, he is not aware of this; there is no conscious understanding. The frustration arises because his drunkenness is fleeting and dependent.

A yogi does not view intoxication negatively. He doesn't regard it as a deviation from his path but as a signpost urging, "more wine." Observing the general pursuit of fleeting intoxication, he sees humanity as essentially inebriated, unaware of their submersion in an ocean of wine. They are surrounded by intoxication but blocked from fully experiencing it due to their limited perception. Observing this, he identifies the issue: there is a waterfall of pure wine, and what you truly seek is to stand under it and be completely drenched. Yet, you approach this abundant source with only a small cup - your body. You try to catch the wine with this cup, but it's too small; the overwhelming force of the waterfall, symbolizing the vibrant force of life and inner experiences, tends to empty your cup rather than fill it. Occasionally, a bit remains, and you savor those moments, but there's immense frustration because you're only tapping into a tiny fraction of what's available, constrained by the belief that you must drink from the waterfall using only the cup of your body and mind.

Nobody has taught you the art of discarding the cup to simply stand and get drenched under that waterfall. Society has gone to great lengths to ensure you cling to the cup. Immense emphasis has been placed on the cup - on identity, name, form, and self-awareness - that you fear abandoning it even briefly to embrace the waterfall fully. A yogi understands this. He recognizes that his own body and mind are what constrain his pure experience of life. This realization is what withdrawing from the senses truly entails.

MIND STUFF

What Patanjali is emphasizing is the need to withdraw from this limited body and mind, turning inward to search for signs of the ultimate and move in that direction. When the senses retract from their objects and begin to imitate the nature of the mind-stuff, this is pratyahara. Withdrawing from the world of senses and emulating the nature of the mind-stuff - what exactly is this "mind-stuff?" It is nothing but the realm you occupy: a mind unburdened by distractions and thoughts. The pure mind is this mind-stuff, the realm of intoxication. Patanjali uses "mind-stuff" to refer to one of the aspects of consciousness, which includes the capacity to think and perceive. Your entire life unfolds within this realm of mind-stuff; not just your thoughts, but your body and actions are also part of this realm. Guarding the entry to this mind-stuff are your senses. By withdrawing from these external guards, you can contemplate the nature of the mind, which Patanjali refers to as mind-stuff. From this arises supreme mastery over the senses. This vigilance, this heightened awareness and alertness, allows a yogi to withdraw from fleeting pleasures. That is why, to those observing from the outside, yoga often seems life-negative.

A yogi might seem almost foolish to outsiders, as he appears to deny his body, his mind, and all life's apparent gifts, spending his time and energy seemingly doing nothing. However, what is invisible to them is the winemaking process underway - a distillation occurring in silence. This distillation cannot be actively performed; it must simply happen. A yogi's role is to create the right conditions, allowing the natural fermentation to occur on its own.

No one fully understands how fermentation occurs. You can't consciously force it, but you know the necessary conditions to facilitate it. Creating these conditions allows fermentation to naturally unfold. This parallels what happens in yoga. What do you do with your mind? What do you do with your body? How do you engage when you withdraw from the external world or when you intellectually grasp the essence of yoga? You are setting up all the essential conditions for fermentation to take place. The ingredients - the stuff of your mind, body, thoughts, and the so-called noise and disturbances of the world - are the raw materials that will be transformed into wine. It's the same the same grapes which, through a bit of transmutation and understanding, become a source of immense joy and pleasure. What you currently perceive as noise, chaos, confusion, pain, and frustration are all in their raw form, needing transformation and fermentation. Yoga is the process of converting everything you recognize as life into intoxication. It transforms pain into pleasure, misery into ecstasy, and the fragmented, limited experiences of your mind and body into a singular, ultimate experience. This process is the essence of yoga, necessitating silence, stillness, control, and awareness - a winemaking process that, someday, you will begin to taste internally.

The fool who watches and ridicules you will never comprehend what you have discovered. He cannot understand the transformation within you because he has denied the possibility his entire life. He has dismissed the Buddha and all enlightened beings, shunning the spiritual quest in favor of a life mired in names and concepts. Yet, deep down, he senses that his life has been unfulfilled, and the only way he might recognize this void is by rediscovering that deeper knowledge himself, by beginning to turn inward. There is no other way to truly grasp the value of yoga and meditation except by diving into your inner world. This intoxication must be tasted and experienced directly. You cannot merely lick the wine bottle and understand its essence - you must open it and drink. However, if you are averse to the idea of drinking, you'll never unseal the bottle. And so, for many, life is lived just on the surface, encircling the wine bottle but never daring to open it due to fear, societal norms, or religious prohibitions.

A yogi gets straight to the point. He asks, "What is the purpose of a wine bottle if not for drinking the wine?" He poses a simple question: "What is the purpose of the human body and mind if not to merge with the ultimate? What is the meaning of human life if not the search for a divine experience?" The quest for divinity, enlightenment, and awakening is the purpose of human life. That is why I have this body, why I possess this awareness, why I understand language, why I can read what Buddha said two thousand five hundred years ago. Why do I even have the capability to do all this? Why am I not simply living and dying like an animal? Why this profound awareness? Why this abundance of music? Why such depth of intoxication? Because that's your purpose - to use all your faculties, abilities, and skills to direct your attention towards the ultimate. All your skills and abilities reach their peak in yoga.

If you think whatever you're trying to accomplish in the world is challenging enough, is stimulating your being, and presents a big enough challenge, try yoga. You will not find an endeavor, an activity, that is more challenging, adventurous, or exhilarating. You have criticized yoga, moved away from it, or not approached it because you've only observed it from a distance. You've only perceived its negatives - asceticism, withdrawal - but not the transmutation, not the fermentation process. From these, supreme mastery over the senses emerges. You don't know what it is to control your senses. You are a slave to them. Mastery comes through non-attachment and recognizing the difference between pure consciousness and its objects. Patanjali gets technical here.

DRUNK ON YOGA

You need a method, a system, or a process to move inward; you cannot venture in blindly. That process is detachment. Consciously, step-by-step, you can withdraw from the world of senses by practicing detachment. The senses are mastered through non-attachment and by observing the distinction between pure consciousness and the object. That is the sutra. Know that you are separate from everything you observe. What you observe is an object; you are the subject. If you can watch something, then you are not what is being watched. Everything that can be observed, including your body, mind, thoughts, and even your breath, belongs to the realm of objects. If you can see it, it is not you. This is challenging news for those who have assumed identities based on what they see, mistaking their observations for their essence.

It is good news for the one who has always known that they are something more. "I'm not just my body. I'm not merely my mind. I am not an accident. There is something deeper to my life." For the one who has begun to look in that direction, they can see that withdrawing from the world of objects - from the world created through observation - eventually leads to the perception of pure consciousness. That distinction, that separation, is what pratyahara is about. You're not withdrawing from the world in a negative sense; you are simply distinguishing between who you are and what you observe. And how do you achieve this? Always remember the watcher. Wherever you go, whatever you do - whether experiencing pain or pleasure, happiness or misery -   place all that in one basket and observe it. Yes, you will experience pain differently from pleasure, but the act of observing is always the same. The watcher does not attempt to alter your pain or happiness; that is your own frustration. The watcher observes pain with the same intensity as pleasure. Ideally, when pain occurs, if it could be ignored, life would seem more peaceful. But the watcher never departs. In times of suffering, he advises, "Watch it." When you can observe during moments of intense pain and pleasure, you can also choose to observe when nothing significant is happening. Whether you're simply walking, sitting quietly, or having a conversation, just maintain focus on the one who is observing.

Slowly, you will begin to realize that this watcher is nowhere near the body. It's as if it's sitting on a hilltop, observing your life. It is not entangled in your misery or your happiness; it is simply observing. And this "he" is not really a "he." We use "he" or "she" just for convenience - it is watching. But because it is your own consciousness, your own essence, we personalize it. Pratyahara is about going against feeding on sense pleasures; not by condemning them, but by understanding and observing them. This is a completely different approach. Condemning sense pleasures only embeds you deeper into them; that's why condemnation has never truly worked. The more we have condemned sense pleasures, the more we have become attached to them. Yoga is the art of practicing withdrawal through observation, through mindfulness. It may seem contradictory in words and concepts: How can observing my sense pleasures lead to transcending them? That is the essence of yoga. You cannot fully grasp it through words alone. When you engage in the practice, when you truly observe, you'll see how this act of observation transforms those ordinary experiences into the perfect wine, the ultimate intoxicant.

DHARANA - FOCUS

After withdrawing your senses from external objects, you bring your scattered energies to a single point - an extraordinarily crucial step that can easily be misunderstood. Focus, awareness, withdrawal, concentration: these words are central to your practice, so each must be fully and contextually understood. Misunderstanding here could be fatal for your yogic practice. You won't literally die, but the "yogi" in you might. The confusion can be overwhelming: "Do I focus? If so, what do I focus on? Am I focusing correctly? If I am merely focusing, then am I meditating? What is the difference between focusing and being aware? Should I focus, or should I be aware? What exactly is concentration?"

You cannot ask these questions somewhere in the middle of your yogic journey. You must ask them early on and have a clear, precise, and concise understanding and definition of what each term means. There's no room for ambiguity. So, Patanjali dedicates quite a few verses to this step of yoga, which he calls "dharana," following the withdrawal from the outer senses. Dharana is the process of fixing the attention of the mind on a single object. Each sutra he provides eliminates one dimension of focusing. For Patanjali, focusing is not just an intermediary process; it is complete in itself. Up until now, whatever you have done was only preparing the stage. Now, the dance begins - the actual process of yoga starts with focus, which defines a yogi.

Living scattered in the world is an ordinary, pointless, meaningless existence where your energies are dissipated every moment. It takes great effort to bring your energies to one point. Yoga is like an atomic explosion within you when you bring all your energies to a single point. It will take time, it will require effort, and you will miss this point again and again. That is your journey - that is the process. But ultimately, yoga is as simple as fixing your attention on a single object. Everything else happens as a consequence of this one effort.

After the preparatory phase, there is really no separation between a yogi and a meditator. Until now, we have discussed yoga because these preparatory steps are often missing in most meditative practices. Most teachers start directly with the mind because they have already gone deep and can clearly see that the mind is the obstacle. They begin working directly on the mind. However, yoga goes a step further. It recognizes that before a meditator can emerge, he must be carved out of the collective, extracted from his routine of activities where he is lost. Only then can he be introduced to the tremendous possibility of awakening. This is where yoga differentiates itself with its preparatory steps. The attitude you bring to the practice, the ferociousness, the one-pointedness, enhances this process. That is why the term "yogi" carries more weight than "meditator."

In fact, we hardly use the word "dhyana," although it's a beautiful term. Dhyana refers to someone in meditation. However, we often use the term "yogi" because a yogi is the personification of inner strength, courage, and is the ultimate symbol of resilience. Except for this distinction between yoga and meditation in the initial phases, everything we discuss from here on will align closely with what a meditation teacher might offer. From this point, Patanjali mirrors Buddha. His methods and processes are in harmony with the meditative school. This is the true essence of yoga. Those who didn't connect with the meditative aspects of yoga deviated and created various yogic schools focused mainly on physical aspects - which often resulted in the physical gymnastics of yoga. They were captivated by the preparatory phase and chose to remain there indefinitely, without turning inward. Once the preparatory phase is complete, the language, the words, and the understanding all require a deep level of intelligence.

If yoga, in its preparatory phases, symbolizes brute strength, willpower, and the ability to disengage from the world and the realm of the senses, from this point forward, a yogi embodies intelligence. He is discerning, observant, and deeply understands each concept introduced to his mind, dissecting and studying their inner meanings.

Dharana is the process of focusing the mind's attention on a single object. The sutra is straightforward - clearly defining focus. It is the act of directing the mind's attention to a single object. Without a specific focus, the concept of focusing loses its meaning. You cannot focus on nothingness; you cannot focus on what isn't there. Focusing on silence or stillness seems unattainable because your primary tool for understanding life is through focusing. You direct your energy toward an object, spending enough time to gain the necessary understanding, mirroring the learning process that occurs in everyday life.

Without channeling your energies into specific activities, actions, or locations at designated times, learning - both intellectual and experiential - is impossible. A scattered mind cannot learn. If you are distracted, with an attention span lasting only a few seconds, it will be difficult to direct your energies to achieve anything meaningful. Forget about mastering yoga - the grandest of quests - even accomplishing simple daily tasks would be a struggle. You would need to battle with your mind and your body due to a lack of focus. Focus is the essential first step in gathering your scattered self. It's necessary because you're often unaware of even your physical location, let alone understanding who you are. Sometimes you're lost in your thoughts, sometimes overly aware of bodily sensations, sometimes you're mentally in your neighbor's house, and at times, you're completely out of this world. You need to reclaim your energies from the myriad experiences in which you've dispersed them - that's where you've hidden yourself. This is why focusing demands effort; naturally, you've led a very scattered life. You understand what focusing is, but its application has been limited to certain activities, and even this skill had to be taught. Someone took the time to teach you the art of focusing, which you eventually learned.

The type of focus required in yoga differs from that in everyday activities, yet in one sense, it is the same - it involves directing your energies to a singular point. Let's look into what it means to gather our energies in one place. This leads to the yogic practice of focusing, which blends concentration with awareness - it's not a simple focus.

Consider the lives of extraordinary individuals, such as successful scientists. A common trait among them is their profound ability to focus, to remain engaged with a single problem for longer than most. This persistence is often what distinguishes a successful scientist from others who haven't made significant breakthroughs. Einstein himself remarked, "I am not particularly intelligent. I am merely passionately curious, and I persist with my problems longer than most." What he meant by persisting is focusing his energies on resolving an issue without giving up.

This brings us to the multifaceted nature of focus: what to focus on, how long to focus, and how to contend with a mind that incessantly seeks distraction. Focusing requires a lot of effort because the mind, by its nature, prefers variety and resists the monotony of concentrating on a single task, like pondering a mathematical equation for hours. This resistance is what a scientist combats.

In this respect, a yogi is similar to a scientist. While the scientist's challenge lies in external problems, the yogi's challenge is introspective - the yogi seeks to understand everything about himself. The required mental faculties - internal strength, dedication, and commitment - are identical. Understanding how focusing functions in the external world can make it easier to apply these principles internally in the practice of yoga.

We can find numerous examples of individuals who have achieved great things through their ability to focus. Take, for instance, Immanuel Kant - not a scientist, but a philosopher. Even in philosophy, a significant degree of focus and awareness is required to unravel life's crucial problems. Philosophical thinking demands sustained attention; you must dwell on a single idea long enough to view it from various angles. This deep focus is what broadens your philosophical understanding.

It is said that Kant was so punctual and systematic that the residents of Königsberg could set their clocks by his daily routine. He was known for his regular visits to a particular pub at lunchtime, where he always ordered the same meal: roast pork and potatoes. The restaurant owner knew Kant's routine so well that by the time Kant walked in, his lunch was already prepared. Kant would eat with total focus and awareness, undistracted by anything else. This routine became so well-known that townspeople would gather just to watch him dine, knowing exactly where he would be at that time.

There's something profound to appreciate here, though it might initially appear trivial or overly mechanical. Kant's regimented lifestyle, which some might view as a waste or overly methodical, actually held tremendous beauty and purpose. He established such a routine to channel all his energies toward his philosophical work, avoiding the distraction of daily decisions. By solidifying his daily habits - knowing exactly where he would eat, what he would wear, and what he would order - he minimized the mental effort spent on routine activities. This conservation of energy allowed him to focus more deeply on his philosophical inquiries. In essence, focusing builds habits, and well-established habits reduce the need for ongoing distractions. This frees up mental resources for more significant pursuits.

The effort you invest in learning to focus is crucial, as it ultimately reduces the need for effort to maintain that focus. Initially, focusing is challenging because you are establishing new patterns and grooves in your thinking. Over time, however, these patterns become ingrained, making focusing easier. This level of focus is essential, especially in the early stages of your inner journey, where you have just detached from the world of senses and are striving to maintain your attention on a single, subtle target. This could be your breath, an imagined center of light, or a point on your forehead - whatever the focus, it must be intense.

Such intensity ensures that your awareness doesn't slip back to the sensory world. You're essentially battling your mind's constant attempts to distract you, which is why your focus must be singular and firmly fixed on one object.

You need to define this process of focusing for yourself, depending on what you're focusing on, how long you're focusing, and the nature of your focus. While focusing means keeping your attention on a single point, in practice, you can't always stick to just one spot. You need a bit more room to let your mind wander a bit; otherwise, you'll explode from the pressure, or you'll just keep failing and getting distracted. So, set clear boundaries for your focus. For instance, if you're focusing on your breath, decide whether you're going to focus on the entire in-breath or the entire out-breath. Watch the whole breath, from the start of the inhale all the way to the start of the exhale. This way, there's no confusion - you know exactly what your focus is. Without setting these boundaries, you'd be like playing darts in the dark, not knowing which point to hit. Define your focusing activity clearly. What does it look like? What does it feel like? And by setting these definitions, you'll know exactly when you lose your focus. That's your first step.

When this process is continuous and uninterrupted, it becomes dhyana. Dhyana is meditation. What Patanjali is highlighting here is significant. He is saying that when your focus is continuous and uninterrupted, it becomes dhyana. We often think that focus and meditation are completely different. Focus requires effort and is used to accomplish tasks in the world, while meditation is about expanding awareness and consciousness, and is inherently relaxing. But how does focusing lead to meditation? In the internal realm, the quality of focusing is different. Here, focusing is always accompanied by awareness. It's not just about focusing, but also about being aware of the one who is focusing. This is the key difference between mere focusing and the kind of focused practice in yoga that evolves into meditation. That's why in yoga, focusing is practiced deliberately, always directed inwardly, minimizing distractions.

FOCUS VS. AWARENESS

Focusing in yoga is a dedicated practice, unlike any other endeavor in life because it involves being aware of the one who is focusing. Even Immanuel Kant, despite developing a perfect routine and rhythm of life, did not become a yogi, a meditator, or reach enlightenment because he did not observe himself while focusing. He was merely focusing. The same goes for Einstein and Newton; their focus helped them solve specific problems, but not the problem of life itself. In contrast, a yogi or meditator brings a completely different dimension to focusing. They are not just watching their breath; they are aware of themselves watching their breath. This doesn't require extra effort, just a conscious remembering. While focusing demands effort, maintaining this dual awareness is about consistent remembrance.

This has been the single biggest confusion in meditation: "What do I do? Give me a technique. Give me a method." But why are you asking for a method? What is a method, and what is a technique? Awareness can never be a technique. Awareness is simply awareness. You are either aware or you are not. How can a technique or a method improve your awareness? You cannot build awareness. Awareness is not about accumulating experiences. It's like a light switch; it's either on or off. There is no dimming. Awareness is a totality in itself. You are either fully self-aware, or you are not. The concept of being partially self-aware doesn't make sense. So, if awareness can't be developed, techniques and methods are essentially for focusing.

All yogic techniques and meditative methods help to bring your distracted mind to one point, but with one crucial addition: while keeping your focus, also subtly watch the one who's focusing. Don't get lost in focusing. This is the single biggest difference between focusing in the world and focusing in yoga. In yoga, you must not lose consciousness or drift into thoughts. If it happens, you bring your attention back. You know when you are not focusing. In the outer world, you can be completely absorbed and still focus on something.

I remember once, during my early years of education, I visited a Japanese car factory. I was doing a project and had been invited to this company. I can still recall this experience vividly: There was a table where four Japanese individuals were standing, intensely focused on a drawing. I was informed that this would be my department for the project and that these gentlemen would assist me. So, I approached and stood there for about twenty minutes. Despite my presence, those four individuals didn't even realize I was there - not because they were Japanese, although their reputed level of focus might have contributed. They were so engrossed, so deeply lost in their work on what they considered a very critical and important part of their job, that they did not notice someone was standing nearby. Once they finished with the drawing, they interacted with me as if nothing unusual had occurred, without even asking how long I had been standing there. They weren't being disrespectful; their focus was so intense that their awareness of their surroundings was almost nil.

Unless something violent or disturbing happens - something truly critical - they wouldn't notice just a person standing there. That's focusing in the world. People understand this as "losing oneself in an activity." However, in yoga, this is not permitted. You choose your object of focus but never lose awareness of yourself. You watch yourself. This awareness eventually expands to become meditation. Initially, focusing brings your energies to one point, and because you are also aware, you gradually become more aware. What we describe as the expansion of awareness is simply you remembering yourself more and more. The awareness is always there; it doesn't need to expand. However, through the practice of focusing, your awareness seems to expand because you are continually remembering to stay aware, undistracted. By focusing the mind on the form, qualities, and purpose of an object, dharana is attained.

Patanjali says that focusing isn't merely about maintaining your attention on a single point. Focusing can be expansive. As long as you can define your area of focus, you're allowed to explore within that space. Focusing means keeping your attention on your defined area, and within that space, you can focus on the form, qualities, and purpose of an object. Whatever you are focusing on, your attention should remain on that object, and your thoughts should revolve around it. When your mind wanders to something else, that's when you know you are deviating. You then need to bring your attention back to the object of your focus. The flow of concentration should be steady and unbroken, like the continuous flow of oil.

Beautiful example: Initially, when you try to focus, it is choppy. You can see the frustration when the objective is to pour oil from one cup to another. It takes a steady hand to do this smoothly. Your hand can be so steady that the flow of oil is continuous without interruption. And that is the ultimate objective of focusing - to become so steady that focusing happens effortlessly. Initially, when you're learning to focus and to be aware, your hand may shake, causing the oil to spill. This is the frustration you must face in yoga. You cannot be a yogi if you cannot accept failure, disappointment, and frustration. These will be your constant companions throughout your journey. It is better to accept failure and the mistakes you'll make early in your yogic journey and internalize it as part of the process. When you lose focus, instead of criticizing or complaining, simply bring your attention back to focusing, because losing focus is natural. Eventually, you will achieve a steady state.

By meditating on the subtle aspects of perception, one attains knowledge of past and future lives. Here, Patanjali starts from the simple act of focusing and suggests that this can lead to an ability to perceive beyond the conventional limits of time. He isn't implying that one can literally see into the past and future. Instead, he's indicating that through focused practice, one's awareness and understanding can expand. Ultimately, this process can lead to the knowledge of everything, utilizing just this single skill of focused attention. Dharana, the practice of sustained concentration, is the initial stage of Dhyana, or meditation.

You don't need to struggle to meditate or get bogged down by various terminologies like "relaxation," "awareness," or "concentration." Think of it simply as focused awareness. If you maintain focus and awareness, you are effectively meditating. Meditation will naturally unfold. You don't need to wrestle with techniques or methods, nor question what your role is in the process. Your primary task is to concentrate your energies at a single point - this is the most challenging part, and it's something only you can do for yourself. The effort you invest in focusing not only leads to meditation but also deepens it, and eventually leads to awakening.

DHYANA - MEDITATION

Time for meditation - a mysterious, enigmatic phenomenon that is at the heart of all transformations. It is something that can never be truly grasped, that can never be truly understood, because in concepts and ideas, the word "meditation" and what you do in meditation is a bundle of contradictions. Dhyana simply means to be. It is not a doing. It is not an action. It is a state of being. The word closest to "dhyana" in English is "meditation," although the word has been used in contexts that have nothing to do with true meditation.

When you say, "I'm meditating on something," know that you're not actually meditating. You cannot meditate on something. You can focus on something. You can even be aware of something. But you cannot meditate on it. Why? Because meditation is not an activity. Meditation is like a line drawn in the sand. It exists only as an absence, not as a presence. You can be in meditation; you can experience the changes that occur during meditation. You can experience deeper states of relaxation through meditation, but they are all defined not by the presence of something but by the absence of something. Experientially, it feels like something is real. However, in reality, those are the moments when nothing is happening. Meditation is non-experience. That is why it is difficult to understand, yet indispensable for self-realization.

When Buddha was asked, "What did you accomplish through all this arduous effort?" "What was your achievement?" Buddha replied, "I have achieved nothing. But let me tell you what I have lost. I have lost fear. I've lost uncertainty. I've lost anger." What he lost is more significant than what he gained. If he were to continue, he might say, "I have lost the mind. I have lost the body." He could not say that because they would not understand. Although he still appeared as a mind and as a body, and they would have seen Buddha getting angry, frustrated, and disturbed, which is a part of the natural flow of the mind and body, internally, he was free from attachment to that suffering, which cannot be seen from the outside. While a non-meditative mind continues to build its identity on its fears and uncertainties, Buddha experienced them momentarily and let them go. He did not carry forward his frustrations from one day to the next.

That is why, if you are observing a Buddha in the moment, you will not be able to tell any difference between him and someone else. This is because the very nature of the mind is to be in a state of agitation, to be in a state of disturbance. So, if he is using his mind to think, to teach, to plan, there will be disturbance, and you can see that disturbance reflected in the body. The body is nothing but the rippling wave of the ocean of the mind. It is the state of the ocean that eventually reflects in the state of the wave. If the ocean is turbulent, the waves are bigger; it's reflected in the body. But if you go just a little deeper and try to understand the true being of the Buddha, you will see that deep down, he is totally detached.

You would only be able to get a sense of this detachment when the ultimate question of life and death is posed. The way a Buddha accepts death, compared to how you accept death, is where you can actually see the difference. It is in moments of such extraordinary importance that you can get a glimpse into the inner world of a Buddha. Consider Jesus on the cross: He had the ability to say, "Forgive these people, for they do not know what they are doing." Only a realized mind - a mind that has become compassion by its very nature, a mind that has lost the fear of death - can say something like that. Those are the rare moments when we can actually see the extraordinary detachment that had become his reality.

You can see this in almost all the Buddhas. They do not fear death. The rest of the time, when they are moving, interacting, and going about their lives, they are just like anybody else. It is not something that is added to their being that separates them, but rather what is taken away. Meditation is a process of dropping things, not accumulating them. It involves letting go of all that you have gathered in sleep, all that does not belong to you. To be free from the afflictions of thoughts, from the desires of the ego, from greed and lust - that is what defines a Buddha, and that is what defines meditation.

THE SEARCH IS INSIDE

You have to approach dhyana as an atmosphere that you're cultivating inside. It is not a search for a thing, nor a search for an experience. It involves taking in the experience of your meditation in its totality and observing the changing weather patterns in the realm you're occupying. It is not about focusing on anything particular, but about understanding the direction you're moving by the changes in the atmosphere. Too many clouds, less light, too much rain - you can identify these. There is no need to categorize this as good or bad; it's just that the atmosphere is heavy with thoughts today. That is the reality of my situation now, but only now. In the next moment, a strong wind could push all these clouds away and reveal the open sky. If I cling to the clouds, if I cling to the idea that I am suffering, filled with thoughts, in pain, then I am drawing out an experience that was meant to last only a while, extending it beyond its necessary timeframe.

That is how you amplify suffering. You amplify your thoughts because you are attached to them, holding onto them longer than necessary. Otherwise, if you observe the entire human phenomenon, it is simply a succession of passing clouds - one of happiness, one of excitement, one of anger, one of disappointment - but nothing remains. Why doesn't anything stay? Because each is a passing cloud. It is not you. It is what you're watching, what you're observing, what you're engaged in at that moment. That is why you can recognize anger as something that is happening to you. If you were not separate from anger, there would be no way to recognize it.

You already know the process of dropping things; you do it unconsciously. No matter how important or impactful an experience is, you know that sooner or later, you will move beyond it. Whether it's pain or pleasure, you cannot hold onto it forever. By the very nature of how your mind functions, you eventually let go of it to embrace new experiences. In meditation, you do this consciously. You become aware of the entire landscape of perception without making any distinctions between what is yours and what is not yours. Everything you perceive belongs to your realm of experiences. Once you are in meditation, there is no such thing as outer and inner.

The whole idea of outer and inner applies only until you reach the point where you have turned inward and are ready for your focus, for your awareness to become meditation. Once your focus begins to expand into awareness, and you start to notice changes in your internal realm, the distinction between inner and outer disappears. Now, everything you perceive, everything you see belongs to you. It is not you, but it belongs to you. It is not happening somewhere outside. If you can hear birds, those birds are singing in the realm of your mind. It is your consciousness resonating with that experience and giving you a perception of those sounds. By its very nature, it cannot be outside. If it were outside, how would you be perceiving it? If I close my ears, I cannot hear it. Thus, I am hearing it through my ears, and then you wander into all the complexities: "Oh, there is an eardrum, and there are sound waves." This is all purely imaginary because it's not part of your experience. In your actual experience, sound is almost a rippling of your consciousness. There is an echoing effect. It's almost like you're in an empty chamber, and sound is bouncing off the walls. You never hear sound as if it is coming from one place and ending at another place.

Experientially, you know that the feeling of listening is totally different from the mechanics of listening. In the mechanics of listening, there is a source and a receiver, and if either the source or the receiver is cut off, there is no listening. But you actually listen to things even when there is no physical source. You listen to your own voice, your own conversation, even when your vocal cords are perfectly at rest. Trust me on this: when you're asleep, your vocal cords are also asleep. You're not actually verbalizing anything. Your tongue is not moving. And yet, you are having a conversation, arguing with someone, hearing your own voice. How is that even possible if listening is purely a mechanical process that requires a source and a receiver? It should be impossible. Not only in sleep, but many times even during the day, you hear things that are not even there.

I'm sure that at least once in your life you have heard something and searched for it, only to realize that it was simply your own mental noise. Even if it has happened just once, that alone proves that listening occurs within a certain dimension. It is not an exchange from the outside to the inside. What you called outside was simply an imaginary separation. It was merely a visual distinction. When you open your eyes, you can see your body and everything happening inside - breathing, digestion, body sensations - you call it "inside." And everything you can observe on the outside, you call it "outside." But the moment you close your eyes, that distinction evaporates. However, you hold on to the idea of separation because you are still attached to the concept of seeing. You are still lost in the world of thoughts.

Once you have sufficiently withdrawn from the world of senses, you are on the path where meditation begins to happen to you. Dhyana occurs because you practiced sense control - pratyahara, and because you focused - dharana. You became an individual who wanted to rely on your own understanding of life. Meditation is the natural consequence of all these processes. Naturally, you will come to realize that there is nothing inside or outside. Everything is simply happening. There are moments when there are fewer happenings, fewer thoughts. The clouds are less dense. They are sometimes transparent - "I can actually see through them and glimpse the clear sky." This happens once in a while because it's not a continuous process; it's not a continuous experience. I dismiss it as momentary imaginations. Because you are so lost in the world of imagination, even reality appears to you as fleeting glimpses of imagination. You're not able to hold onto it. It is only through steady practice that you eventually realize that these glimpses were actually the open sky revealing itself, only hidden behind the cloud of thoughts.

Patanjali says, "When dharana becomes effortless and continuous, it transforms into dhyana." It is the same faculty of focusing, the same faculty of awareness, which was intermittent before and interfered with by thoughts. When this becomes continuous and steady, when it flows without any interruption, that focusing eventually leads to meditation. You cannot "do" meditation; you cannot "practice" meditation, but you can create the conditions for it to happen. This is how it has always happened. Because it is a happening, there is no way to teach it directly. There is no way to give direct instructions to someone to make them meditate. You have to beat around the bush. You have to approach it from the sides, because what you are pointing to, what you are making someone aware of, is the absence of all that noise that is stopping them from perceiving themselves.

Meditation is a natural state of your being. Before you took birth, before assuming this body, before getting attached to this mind, you were in an eternal state of meditation. Meditation was your very nature. You lived in that state beyond time, which means, for eternity, a part of you is older than the earth, older than the stars, older than our entire observable universe combined. Your silence precedes everything else in the universe because silence need not be created. It does not require any evolutionary process. It does not depend on anything. It need not take birth, and it need not die. Silence is eternal. Silence is its own reality, standing by itself, all alone. The day you connect to that silence, you become a part of that eternity. Even one glimpse of that emptiness, that silence, that stillness, introduces you to the eternal nature of your being.

Of course, because your thoughts are still powerful, you cannot hold onto it. That is the frustration. But it's only a matter of time before you become more and more absorbed in that experience of stillness and silence because that is your very nature. Whether you want it or not, you are moving in that direction. You only have to identify how you are disturbing that silence, disturbing that stillness. You are only doing it with your thoughts. There's nothing physical there that is blocking; there's no actual brick wall except for an imaginary one that is your mind and body.

Steady focus on a single object, on a single activity, withdrawing all your awareness and attention from the outside and onto that one thing, that steady focus eventually expands into awareness and becomes meditation. There will come a moment when the one who's focusing and the one who's watching the one who's focusing become separate. That is the moment the meditator is born. That is the moment beingness is recognized. That is the moment the doing has dropped. It has not disappeared; it is still there. There is still someone sitting there and focusing. There is still someone thinking about that process. There is still someone there frustrated that he's unable to meditate. But quietly, you can observe there is someone else who is watching all this without being troubled by any of this. That presence just emanates from the depths of your being. What was hidden, now that you have quietened your mind enough, begins to reveal itself. You didn't have to create meditation. You didn't have to chase after it. You didn't have to use any special or unique techniques. You only had to be rooted in the present moment.

That is what Patanjali calls focusing. Literally, focusing is another word for being here and now. If you can remain in the here and now long enough, everything that is supposed to happen will happen. The only question is, can you hold onto this simple idea of being here and now without getting rejected, without getting frustrated, without giving up? As long as you're not giving up, all the possibilities for your enlightenment are right there. You don't have to create them. There is something that is moving in front of the screen of your mind continuously, uninterruptedly; now that has to be stopped. Your incessant desiring, your world of fears and frustrations, your world of uncertainty, your world of excitement and engagement - everything that you recognize as your world, whatever that might be, has to stop. You have to find that space between two thoughts. Buddha is simply the one who has learned how to stop. That is his life. Now, he can stop at will. What is greater power? Is it to stop something that is happening on the outside or is it to stop your own thought process that is tormenting you? That ability to have control over this continuous flowing stream that never stops, to figure out a way to stop that, is meditation, is dhyana.

There is a story in the life of Buddha. Although this story is narrated as a true story, when you listen to it, you will understand that it is more or less allegorical. However, it could also be true, as this was two thousand five hundred years ago, and people like this might have existed. There was a man named Angulimala, which means "garland of fingers." Angulimala was terrorizing the neighborhood where Buddha lived. His habit or his lifestyle was unique, quite different from the lifestyles we recognize now. He loved killing people, cutting off their fingers, and making them into a garland. His accomplishment was gathering these fingers, which is why he was called Angulimala.

It is said that one day Angulimala happened to meet Buddha. They looked at each other and stopped. Buddha stopped because he saw something that he could influence. He could immediately see that there was something wrong with this man. He had fallen. He had done something that he wasn't supposed to do. He stood there as a symbol of violence, which is directly opposed to Buddha's philosophy of love, compassion, and non-violence

Angulimala angrily stops in his tracks because, for the first time, he sees a man who has no fear in his eyes. Usually, people would freeze in terror at the sight of him, a man adorned with a garland of fingers and probably carrying a hatchet. He's used to seeing terror; he's seen people scream and run in fear. But now, he observes a man who simply stops and looks at him, showing no sign of fear. Angulimala has killed enough people to know that this man is not afraid.

Angulimala looks at Buddha and says, "Stop." Buddha responds, "I have stopped. It is you who are yet to stop." This statement hits Angulimala from a totally different dimension. He's not only fearless; he's telling me to stop. And he's not telling me to stop walking; he's telling me to drop everything I've been doing.

How is this man able to say this with such serenity, with such calmness? It is said that Buddha's words transformed Angulimala. He dropped his hatchet, threw off his garland of fingers, and decided to become Buddha's disciple. His life was transformed in that very moment.

There are two ways of looking at this story: One way is to take it literally. Literally, the story seems unbelievable. Firstly, consider a man whose job, whose work, whose life is to kill and make a garland of fingers - why would someone do that? Secondly, given his rage and terror, it is unlikely he would have paused to recognize the fearless nature of Buddha. He might have reacted violently, just as if you encounter a wild animal: whether you are enlightened or not doesn't matter. The animal reacts based on its instinctive state at that moment. For instance, standing in front of a hungry lion, whether you are serene and calm doesn't matter - the lion sees only meat, whether moving or not. So, literally, the story is hard to believe. But figuratively, allegorically, it is a beautiful, enchanting story.

THE POWER OF SILENCE

Angulimala represents your mind. Buddha represents silence. This story depicts the encounter between the terrorizing mind and silence. Your mind is often lost in pointless, meaningless activities, symbolized by Angulimala's desire to kill people and make a garland out of their fingers. It's not only viciously brutal but utterly pointless. It addresses the ego, the desire of the ego. The ego doesn't care about its actions as long as it is being glorified, as long as it can feel powerful. Angulimala found his power by killing the helpless. His ego was satisfied in that process. That is the mind. The mind destroys things, creates havoc, both inside and outside, in pursuit of the garland of fingers - a garland of false appreciation - just so that it can feel important. The mind does not realize that it is not real. It does not know that it is an illusion. It must hold onto its illusions, and it does this by engaging in foolish actions.

It is only silence that can stun the mind. It is only silence that can stop the mind. Nothing else can. Try anything, and the mind will simply assimilate it. The mind will overpower that and make it a part of itself. That is the actual meaning of the story. The mind destroys any attempt to stop it and uses that attempt for ego gratification, ego satisfaction. If you want the mind to become meditative without practice, without effort, without gradually introducing it to silence, it takes the idea of meditation and turns it into a garland, then starts using it to preach to others.

Buddha's words, Jesus' words - while they are meant to introduce you to silence - religion has used them as a garland for the ego. Literally, these words are used to inflate the egos of both the speakers and the listeners. What else is a religious game, if not for the inflation, the expansion of the ego? It is silence that can put an end to all this nonsense. An internal experience of silence becomes a mirror reflecting the violence of the mind. The mind is vicious, violent, and destructive. Buddha can see that. The destruction visible in the outside world pales in comparison to the true capabilities of the mind in realms of destruction. The mind is capable of great destruction; it can destroy things externally and internally. It can destroy inner peace, quietness, your ability to simply be, and even your own true self-identity. The mind is a destroyer, which is symbolically represented by Angulimala, while Buddha is the personification of silence.

You have to start from the mind because that's where you are. This is the challenging part of meditation. Before meditation can happen, you must confront this monster. You must deal with its stupid, ignorant ways. You have to sit through watching all that nonsense. It's even harder because it has all happened through you. You have attached yourself to these activities. You have generated these thoughts. Your self-identity is intermixed with these. That is the challenging part of meditation. That is why you need focusing. That is why you need dharana. One-pointed focus can bring this raging storm to a point of stillness from where you can observe it.

First comes the restraining of this monster, which happens through focusing. Then, as that focusing deepens, meditation will occur. In meditation, the mind becomes absorbed only in the object of meditation, as if devoid of its own nature. What Patanjali is saying is that there is the mind and what the mind is doing. Meditation happens when your focus and awareness shift from the object to the subject - from what you're doing to who is doing it, from what the mind is doing to the mind itself. That is the moment when you become aware of the presence that is your mind, the presence that is your being.

Your mind is not something totally different; it's not a mechanical entity. It is your pure being. When it is lost in thoughts, we call that mind. When the focus and awareness shift from the contents of the mind to the mind itself, to the realm itself, then a settling occurs. A recognition happens of the presence of something that isn't disturbing you - something silent, still, nourishing you, holding you up.

That shift is the transition from chaos to clarity, from the noise of the mind to the silence of being, where you become absorbed in the very process of observation. It is a magical experience that you cannot force; it will just happen. As you keep watching, there will come a moment when you lose interest in what you're watching. Despite trying to maintain your focus on one thing, your mind has interfered so much that you've inevitably observed many things. After a while, you become exhausted from watching these things. You've seen too many thoughts, too many experiences. Eventually, a moment arrives when you are utterly disinterested in what you're watching, but your practice of watching has strengthened so much that your attention shifts from what you're watching to the one who is watching. You become absorbed in the mind itself. Dhyana is the uninterrupted flow of awareness towards the chosen object.

When your focus becomes uninterrupted, it evolves into dhyana. Dharana was always there, but because that focusing was not continuous, your attention was being diverted. Anything disruptive or not moving smoothly will draw your attention. For example, when you're driving, as long as your car is running smoothly, you're not particularly focused on driving. You're not thinking about it. But suddenly, if your car starts jerking, no matter where you are - you need to refocus because there is a problem. Your focus isn't continuous; it's a challenge that you're still solving. You just want to watch, but something is preventing you from watching consistently. It's as if someone is intermittently applying the brakes, or like you're driving and someone suddenly covers your eyes. You have to remove their hands to see where you're going, and just as you begin to drive smoothly again, someone covers your eyes once more.

That's the frustration in meditation. You simply want to see what's happening, but your mind resists, saying, "I don't want you to see." You find yourself constantly battling with this mind. Eventually, you will learn to see through the mind. You won't fight with it anymore. You think, "Okay, you can close my eyes, because I'm not using them to see now. I'm using my consciousness, my aliveness. Yes, you can close my eyes. You can even block the road. I don't care because you cannot block my seeing, since my seeing comes from the seer within. I'm not seeing with the 'eye'; I'm seeing with the 'I'." The mind can do whatever it wants. It can continue to be noisy, but now your seeing is steady. Your focusing is continuous. Now, you don't even need an object to focus on; focusing has become an entity unto itself. That moment, that experience where you have transcended the disturbances of the mind, where your awareness and attention are continuous - that state of being, that experience, that atmosphere, is what is called meditation.

In the state of dhyana, the mind flows continuously toward the object of meditation without any interruption. Once you are absorbed in meditation, once you are absorbed in the process of watching, you can then focus on anything uninterruptedly. Now, the choice is yours. You can decide what to focus on and for how long. With this ability to focus, you can start going deeper and deeper, focusing on subtler things, until you ultimately place your focus on the subtlest of things - those that you cannot see, cannot experience, and that none of your senses can grasp - yet you can maintain your awareness on them. When you can be aware of nothing, you have arrived. That is Nirvana. Now, you are there. Your focusing is there. Your watching is there. Your awareness is there, but there is nothing to watch. There's nothing to focus on, no mind to fight with, and no body sensations to distract you. You are there as the purest form of yourself, you without any ideas of you. You cannot imagine what this "you" feels like because you are always intertwined with thoughts. That is why enlightenment is extraordinarily simple and yet almost impossible to define. When it happens, you will know.

SAMADHI

Once you are firmly rooted in the awareness of yourself - what is recognized as self-absorption - where the one who is focusing, the one who is aware, the one who is watching, has taken center stage, you can clearly recognize and feel the presence. Everything else rises and falls in the presence of that presence. The ultimate reality is just a presence. It has no boundaries, no limitations. It is non-physical, does not occupy space, and is not bound by time. That is why defining presence is challenging. When you talk about presence, you typically identify it with your mind and body. You seldom consider that the way you are present is exactly how all other things are present. Each individual experiences the same presence. I'm not saying they experience presence in the same way; I'm saying they experience the same presence. Presence doesn't need to divide itself to enter each human being separately. There is no need for presence to take birth as a seed, grow, and become you. By the very nature of what presence is, it is either there, or it isn't.

There is no question of presence starting as something small and getting bigger because the way you were present as a child is the same as when you are an adult; the presence has not changed. You are not in a new presence; your body has changed, your mind has changed, your thoughts have changed. In fact, everything has changed except for that presence. It is only that presence that you're able to hold on to and say, "This is me." This presence never loses itself in thoughts. It never diminishes. It's always there. That is why there is no fear of going to sleep and waking up, fearing that you might forget yourself. You can go to sleep confidently, without any fear that when you wake up, you are still you because it is really not you who's waking up. Actually, the one who goes to sleep and the one who wakes up are totally different. Something has changed in your mind. Something has changed in your body.

Let us take an example, albeit a gruesome one. Imagine you go to sleep - it's just an example, so don't be alarmed. You're asleep, and for whatever reason, someone decides to amputate one of your hands. They do it so you are unaware, administering enough anesthesia to keep you asleep during the procedure. Now, you don't know your hand is missing because you are blissfully asleep. When you wake up in the morning, how do you wake up? Do you wake up as someone who's missing a hand, or do you wake up as you and then realize one of your hands is missing? It's always the latter. What does that mean? It means that in your sleep you were complete. Just because your hand was cut off, nothing inside was cut off. Your presence was not even touched. Your presence didn't register the missing hand. Most operations that involve severe physical intervention are possible only because of this quality of presence - you can set it aside and just operate on the body. Then, you reintroduce the body to that presence. Well, now you recognize that something has changed in your body, but you are the same. That is why you fall, get up, experience moments of joy, pain, and betrayal, but you always pick yourself up. You are never totally lost.

So what has happened? You wake up in the morning, and when you wake up, you are the same individual as always. It's the same way you've woken up your entire life, except maybe a few thoughts are different, connected to what you were dreaming about. Other than that, the process of waking up, the process of identifying yourself in the morning - "I am up" - or whatever you tell yourself from that moment when you become self-aware, that is part of your life. That waking up itself is always the same, and it is not only the same for you but also for every other human being, for every other creature because presence is not divided. It is the same presence that fills the whole universe. Creatures take birth and die in that presence. Like waves in the ocean, they come and go.

CONSCIOUS SLEEPING

The reason you decided to embark on a yogic journey, the reason you chose to withdraw from the world of senses, and the reason you've spent enormous amounts of time and energy focusing, concentrating, and meditating is to connect with the pure presence that you have always been. Literally, what you have accomplished in all these years of yoga is learning the art of conscious sleeping. Yes, it is a great blow to the ego. You thought you were accomplishing the greatest of things. Now, you're being told that you've only achieved wakeful sleep. However, this is because you don't understand how tremendous a phenomenon wakeful sleep is, how fulfilling, transformative, and transcendental an experience it is. It is the ultimate experience: to be fully at rest, your body in a state of non-disturbance, your mind tranquil, sleeping like a baby, yet consciously watching this sleep. How can this be an ordinary experience? How can this experience not fulfill you completely from the inside? How can it not introduce you to your immortal nature?

Think about it: You've always seen yourself as a body. Criticism of the body felt like criticism of you. Appreciation of the body felt like your own appreciation. All that you've accomplished, you've done using your mind and body, and you are recognized for that. But you know that sooner or later, you will die. You can do nothing about it. You cannot hold on to the body; you cannot hold on to the mind, and that has been your greatest frustration. Despite all your accomplishments, you remain no closer to understanding or controlling death - the inevitable end of both your body and your mind.

Now, for the first time, you're sitting fully absorbed in your own true nature. Your body is just there like a shadow, with eyes closed, breathing exactly as it would when you are asleep. It moves rhythmically, just as in sleep. Every inch of your body is asleep. You can see it. The only difference is, you are asleep while sitting still. There is no effort needed to hold your body still. Once you become identified with consciousness, and that consciousness is detached from the body, whatever position you leave the body in, it will maintain. The fear that if you lose consciousness or awareness you'll fall is because losing consciousness for you has meant being lost in thoughts. In meditation, you don't lose consciousness; you become consciousness. You are so absorbed in the experience of being that your body maintains its position because there's no one to interfere with it now. It is just an image. That is why it does not fall over.

If the body were truly substantial, then yes, there would be a danger. "If I go into Samadhi, what if my body falls?" That is the last thing you need to worry about because your body is a projection of your mind, a self-image. An image will always maintain its last known position and place. It is only objects that move. Images don't.

If there is a painting, whatever is on that painting will always remain. If there is a person depicted in the painting, there's no fear he's going to walk away. He'll always be there. Why? Because it's an image. It was created by a higher consciousness, by a human being, not by another painting or from within the painting itself. That painting was created from outside, from awareness, from watchfulness. The only thing missing in this experience of connecting with your pure self is that you are so attached to that painting, so entangled in it, that you have completely forgotten you created it. That painting has become your complete identity. It is a three-dimensional painting where things move around. Your body moves around, but the actual mover is outside - it is the presence. When you connect with that presence, you are simply leaving the image to itself, just as you leave the painting to itself. If you don't interfere with the painting, the image will hold itself. Likewise, if you don't do anything with the body, it will hold itself. In fact, this is an indication that it is ripe - you are ready to drop your body consciousness.

ABSOLUTE STILLNESS

The final stage of yoga occurs after the body freezes. What do I mean by "body freezes"? Until this point, maintaining a certain posture required some effort. For example, sitting straight requires a bit of effort to prevent slumping or falling asleep. You are fully aware of where your hands, head, neck, and the rest of your body are. When you move, even though the instructions come from within and are carried out almost thoughtlessly, the body responds. There is no lag between thinking about moving your right hand and it moving. So, any internal movement, if not consciously monitored, reflects in the body's movement. That's why if you stop observing the body and drift into thoughts, your body also drifts and may no longer maintain a steady posture.

Literally, what is the difference between a body that is sitting still and one that is lying down? The body that is sitting still is holding itself, trying to remain present, aware of what's happening here and now. In contrast, a body lying down may have lost its consciousness and drifted away, which is why it cannot maintain its position. In samadhi, a separation occurs between the object you're observing, which is your body, and the subject, which is you. Before this separation happens, your body becomes absolutely still. It freezes to the point where, if you try to move it using normal, everyday thoughts like you used to, it will not respond.

Because the disconnection is happening, your body begins to seem like an entity separate from you, as though it does not belong to you. Now, nothing is automatic. To control this body, you need to act consciously. You have to identify with the body again to move it. This will occur after the absorption phase, after enlightenment, when you become aware of the body again and it begins to move. However, in that moment when the body is freezing, let it be. There's no need to fear being unable to move. It might feel as though someone is holding you, and every part of your body is trapped, unable to move.

Now, the reason why you feel this is because your identification has shifted from the moving body to the still presence, causing the body to freeze. Then begins a magical process of deep self-absorption, where the object of your awareness and focus becomes the subject itself, because there's nothing else to be aware of, nothing else to watch. For a while, you might still play with a few thoughts - even though your body is frozen, these thoughts linger, which is why it takes a bit more time for the disconnection to fully happen. While this experience might sound scary, you've gradually reached this place through steps, and because it has happened to you again and again, you are prepared for it.

Of course, nothing can fully prepare you for the ultimate experience of Samadhi. What I've described - the body freezing, the separation, and deep self-absorption - are just precursors to Samadhi. These are the aspects we can talk about. Patanjali suggests that Samadhi is attained through deep and sustained contemplation of an object, with complete absorption and no sense of individuality. He isn't defining Samadhi directly; he's discussing what happens just before reaching it, how you would experience readiness for it. This readiness manifests as deep and sustained contemplation, where, in this case, the "object" is your own self - though, truly, there is no object, just consciousness aware of itself. It hasn't yet collapsed back onto itself, but you are there, with nothing left to watch or observe. In this state of complete absorption, there is no sense of individuality because everything that you identify as "you" is linked to your mind and body. As pure presence, you are not an individual; you are not the person you thought you were. You are simply that pure presence, the same presence illuminating all other forms of life.

Just think about the magnificence of this experience. In a single moment, you transition from being an individual - limited, confused, uncertain, confined to body and mind - to becoming a presence that permeates everything. You become the source of all life and light, truly embodying your deepest self without any individuality, without any defining qualities. This is why such presence is referred to as Nirguna Brahman. 'Brahman' signifies the vast expanse, and 'Nirguna' means without qualities. You become Nirguna Brahman: a pure, vast mind, unattached to anything, liberated from the constraints of a limited existence bound to the mind and body. What you experience in that moment of deep contemplation is samadhi, the stage just before the ultimate explosion. Yes, you are Nirguna Brahman, in deep awareness of your true self, with no body, no mind - yet, there's still something. One last thing remains. When that finally drops, the explosion happens. This is where words fail to capture the essence of the experience. No one can truly describe it; they can only guide you toward it.

Think about it. There was a time when you didn't even believe in an inner dimension. You lived entirely on the outside, relying completely on scriptures and acquired knowledge as you began to turn inward. Now, you've discovered an entire world of experiences. You've found peace, certainty, stillness, and silence. If you've come this far, then the ultimate explosion is only a matter of time. You can't force it to happen, nor do you need to fear that it won't. If so much has already unfolded, the rest will follow. It always has. Once you've achieved that steadiness of observation, it's the same process of focusing that has perfected and deepened.

It's the same process that eventually leads to the ultimate liberation. In the state of samadhi, only the object of meditation shines forth, devoid of its specific characteristics. Consider the profundity of this statement. When you are deeply self-absorbed, what you observe is present but lacks qualities. What is a body without characteristics? It ceases to be a body. What is a mind without qualities? This is the final image of your mind and body that you transcend. Yet, in deep self-absorption, you aren't actually experiencing the mind and body; you perceive them only as distant shadows. You are wholly engrossed in experiencing your true self. In samadhi, the focus itself becomes the object of meditation, so perfect and pointed that it no longer requires a separate entity to focus on.

DEFINING THE EXPLOSION

This is where each enlightened teacher varies in their explanation of samadhi, their explanation of enlightenment. There remains something subjective in that experience, something personal that each individual brings because they are still present. Almost all descriptions of enlightenment detail how an individual perceives those moments just before the enlightenment occurs. For Buddha, it was an experience of nothingness. Remember, when Buddha speaks of nothingness, he is not describing the actual experience of enlightenment itself. No one has ever fully articulated the experience of enlightenment because it's the moment when the explosion of understanding happens - beyond definition. You can only discuss what occurs just before or after it. Buddha isn't defining enlightenment per se; he's outlining his approach to reaching it. For him, before that explosive moment, there was no body, no mind - nothing was there. That is the last thing his consciousness registers because during the explosion, there's nothing to record. If there's nothing to register, how can anyone describe enlightenment as a specific thing? It's always about the moments just before awakening.

The attitude you bring to meditation, whether you approach it through the path of knowledge, love, or devotion, significantly impacts your experience just before awakening. Were you filled with terror or certainty? This distinction shapes each enlightenment experience uniquely. For instance, in the Abrahamic traditions, descriptions of enlightenment or divine encounters - often referred to as meeting God - are typically portrayed as violent experiences. Figures like Abraham, Moses, David, and Jeremiah experienced these moments with a sense of terror. This was because there was no structured meditative method guiding them; their enlightenment was achieved primarily through a path of deep devotion. Their profound belief in something higher and beyond was what ultimately pushed them over the edge.

These men were very different from modern individuals. Religion, divinity, and God were inseparable parts of their lives. They were born into these belief systems. So, deep down, whatever they were searching for, they believed they were searching for God. They did not define their experience as systematically as Buddha did. Abraham would be horrified if he heard that Buddha described enlightenment using the word "nothingness," because for him, it was about meeting the divine - an ultimate experience, an ultimate communion. You are encountering something spectacularly grand, something much bigger than yourself. In your mind, you have projected this entity to be immense, and you have revered it deeply. Just before the explosion happens, you are filled with terror - the terror of losing your body, the terror of losing your mind. Then the explosion happens. That is why, when they come back to the body, they recall their enlightenment experience as terrifying. Even Mohammed said, "When I started hearing the verses of the Quran, my body began to tremble. I was shivering. In fact, I said, Enough, I cannot take it anymore. I am just an illiterate fool; why are you pouring this much knowledge, this much wisdom into my being? I cannot handle it."

Now, what is he saying? He's describing that moment when his individual identity was yielding to something grander. Mohammed did not approach awakening like Buddha did, in a systematic, step-by-step process like a Zen master or Lao Tsu would. If you look at all the awakened Zen masters, there is no mention of terror. They describe enlightenment in very ordinary terms. They don't portray it as a spectacular event because they are so aware of the steps, and they have approached it so scientifically and methodically that even the explosion, when they recall it, is perceived as something inevitable. It was merely the relinquishment of the mind and body. Yes, the experience was spectacular - it is no ordinary experience - but they describe it in ordinary terms. Those who have approached it through the path of devotion speak of it in terms of a spectacular experience. Yet, they are all discussing a real experience.

Now, who isn't talking about a real experience? Who is merely making a fool of himself and others? It's the one who parrots the words of these individuals without a single drop of understanding of what they are talking about. All these so-called preachers, popes, and fathers - these so-called religious men - are merely repeating the words. They have no conception of the experience. That is why they can repeat these words with so much confidence. They can create all kinds of illusory concepts of heaven and hell and populate these realms with various ideas. They do this with confidence because they know, deep down, it's all a lie. They know, experientially, that what they are defining is not how things truly are.

See, you will be confident at two stages in your life. One is when you are possessed with some extraordinary knowledge, experiential knowledge that fills you completely and transforms your life. That is one moment where you will be totally confident - like Milarepa's confidence, Meera's confidence. Then there'll be a moment when you know nothing. You have to fabricate an idea to survive; you know the very foundation is false. Then again, you'll be very confident because you know it's a total lie. It is only in the middle where you are uncertain, possessing a little bit of your experience and a little bit of conceptual understanding. That is why you are uncertain. If you see a person who's uncertain, who's not sure about heaven and hell, who's not sure about whether you will be on the right hand side of God or the left, who's not sure what type of oil is used to fry you in hell - when you're not sure, that means you are somewhere in the middle between truth and lies. You're trying to understand. But a religious person, so filled with just the idea of what he's talking about, makes no effort whatsoever to understand if what he's saying is true. He can do it very confidently because he does not come anywhere near the truth. A story comes to mind:

A group of professors were invited onto a plane. When the door closed and the plane was about to take off, all the professors were informed that their students had built the plane. All the professors rushed toward the plane door, trying to escape and survive, except for one professor who remained seated with much confidence and calmness. Someone asked him why he wasn't trying to escape. The professor answered with confidence that he was sure the plane wouldn't fly.

A religious man knows there is no heaven or hell. That's why he's not afraid to preach it to you. That's why he can confidently stand on the podium and talk about it for hours on end. He knows there's no way you can verify it. Imagine if heaven and hell were real. Then he would need to know experientially what happens there before he could speak so confidently. What if someone who had been to hell came back and challenged him, saying, "No, I didn't see this in hell the last time I was there." Because the whole concept is an illusion - a drama, a game - these individuals can lie with confidence. And they don't even consider themselves liars because, to them, it's the truth. You cannot judge a teacher or a master solely by their confidence. You need to scrutinize their words, to see if they make sense. If confidence alone were the criterion, then you would likely be misled - and many people have been misled by such confident preachers. But deep down, they know they haven't taught you anything real. That's where their confidence comes from. Buddha's confidence is different. It stems from an experience, an experience of samadhi.

How is Patanjali able to provide such a fantastic, systematic step-by-step journey into the inner realm? It is so precise - every word he uses, every sentence he speaks. Someone who has experienced that something on the inside knows he is speaking the truth, and he knows that these words come from experience. He's not parroting someone else's words; he's sharing his own interpretation, his own experience of the Yoga

Sutras. He didn't invent the Yoga Sutras, but his commentary illuminates them. In the highest state of samadhi, the mind transcends all mental constructs and identities, leading to the realization of the true self. Watch carefully what he's saying: in the highest state of samadhi. So samadhi was not the ultimate; there was still something waiting to happen.

While in Hinduism, samadhi is regarded as the ultimate experience, in actuality, samadhi is a state - a place where you are deeply self-absorbed, where there are no ripples in your mind. That is why the word 'samadhi,' where 'sama' means equal and 'dhi' refers to the mind, literally means there are no waves - no waves of thoughts, no waves of body sensations - just pure awareness, pure watchfulness. And even that deepens. From here, it all happens quickly; sometimes in the very same session where you're sitting, you touch samadhi, go deep, and the explosion happens. Sometimes you sit in samadhi and come back to body consciousness. There is no one way of defining exactly when awakening or enlightenment happens - it happens differently for different people, but samadhi indicates you are close - the explosion is not far away. In fact, samadhi itself is such an exhilarating experience, occurring at the end of your arduous journey of yoga, after you have struggled with the mind, wrestled with the body, become exhausted, frustrated, and a deeper settling has happened - that is when samadhi occurs.

Samadhi will not happen initially. It should not be confused with other stages; some subjectivity is allowed in yoga based on how you view it, and your individual experiences may differ. However, broadly, the stages of yoga are always the same. Just because you approach meditation differently doesn't mean you will experience samadhi first and then focus next. The steps are precise. In the highest state of samadhi, the mind transcends all mental constructs because, ultimately, what is the mind? It is the structures, the boundaries that you have created for yourself. You have transcended all those boundaries and identified with the self, leading to the realization of the true self. What is the true self? That presence, that undivided presence. There is no other journey like the inward journey. If going inward is the ultimate of all journeys, then yoga is the ultimate of all methods.

There has never been, nor will there ever be, another method or technique that is more grand, more scientific, more precise, or more illuminating than the path of yoga. You can invent your own methods and techniques, but they will always fall within the framework of yoga. What Patanjali has provided is the complete pathway to awakening - nothing is missing. He starts from the outside: your actions, your activities, your desires, and leads you to the experience of your pure, true self. Now, if there is one thing in life to be enthusiastic about - one thing that can simultaneously transform you from the inside out and answer all your questions - it is yoga. Even the word "enthusiasm" etymologically means having the divine enter into the worshipper who believed that he became one with the divine. The word itself means to become one with the divine. What else are you searching for in life? Some enthusiasm, some exhilaration? The very definition of the word signifies a search for the ultimate. You can call it divine, the self, Brahman, or nothingness, but that is the greatest enthusiasm - to merge your individual identity with the universal identity. This experience answers the most important questions: Who are you? Why are you here? What is the purpose of your life? What is the meaning of your life? Now, knowing what yoga and its methods can do for you, how can you turn your back on it? How can you not pursue this path?

Only if you are so lost in life's complications, so utterly ignorant, and afraid of confronting yourself, might you fail to embrace yoga. If there's any courage in your heart, any longing, if even a single brain cell of intelligence remains, you would recognize yoga as your ultimate path. Yoga transcends religion and community, encapsulating the totality of steps leading to awakening. It embodies meditation, mindfulness, control of the senses, focusing, awareness - the entire process, presented without fluff or distraction, just pure steps. You deserve to know the truth of your life; it is your right. Without this pursuit, your life lacks purpose and meaning. This isn't about directing your attention outward as religions might, but inward - urging you to search for yourself. This purity, this utility, this illuminative quality of Patanjali's words aims solely to bring you back to yourself, to free you from all limitations and bondages, to give you a taste of your true essence. There is nothing grander than this.

Whether you are an experienced meditator or just beginning your journey, ultimately, if you want to understand yourself, you have to engage with yoga. The sooner, the better. You'll have more energy and enthusiasm to pursue it, and the ability to handle the challenges it presents more effectively. But at any stage of your life, when you're introduced to this knowledge, when you become aware of yoga, if you are watchful enough, intelligent enough, and courageous enough, you would drop everything else you're doing to understand the path of yoga - the path to your highest self.

About Nirvana

Originally from India, our teacher, Nirvana, embarked on his professional journey in the corporate sector shortly after completing his college education. However, at the age of 24, he realized there was a deep void within him that material achievements could not fill. Yearning for inner tranquility and a sense of purpose, he made the courageous decision to move away from home, leave his job, rent a modest room, and dedicate himself to the pursuit of meditation.

Devoting several years to intense meditation, Nirvana experienced a profound spiritual awakening that forever transformed his life. Motivated by this newfound understanding, he eagerly began sharing his experiences through various programs and retreats. In 2017, he traveled to the United States with one of his students, and upon arrival, he intuitively knew he had found the right place to sow the seeds of consciousness and awareness.

Nirvana Foundation is a nonprofit organization dedicated to providing individuals with opportunities to explore meditation and self-awareness through books and programs. Nirvana speaks twice a day, and his talks are recorded and transcribed by his students. These transcripts are ultimately compiled into books for publication. Currently, our teacher resides and teaches in Tennessee, where the development of the first Nirvana meditation retreat is underway.

Share Your Thoughts

If this book has touched your life, illuminated your path, or opened new avenues of thought and introspection, consider sharing your experience. Your review on Amazon will help us reach others who are searching for answers. Your reflections, insights, and experiences can light the way for fellow seekers on the path to Awakening.

Books by Nirvana

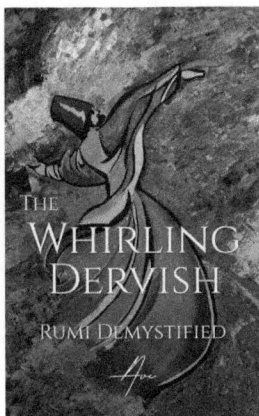

ISBN: 978-1962685009

ISBN: 979-8852311207

ISBN: 979-8392250196

ISBN: 979-8374196740

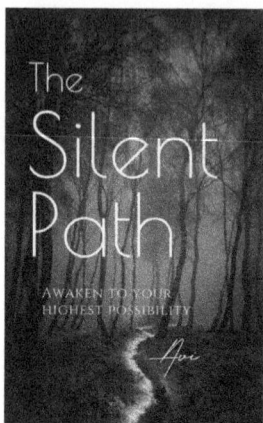

The
Silent
Path

AWAKEN TO YOUR
HIGHEST POSSIBILITY

Avi

ISBN: 978-0578637068

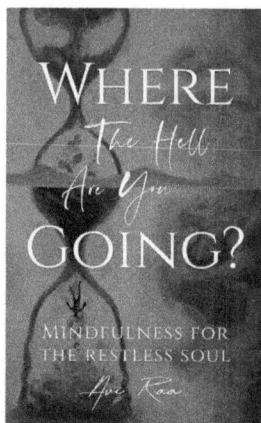

WHERE
The Hell
Are You
GOING?

MINDFULNESS FOR
THE RESTLESS SOUL

Avi Roa

ISBN: 978-1962685023

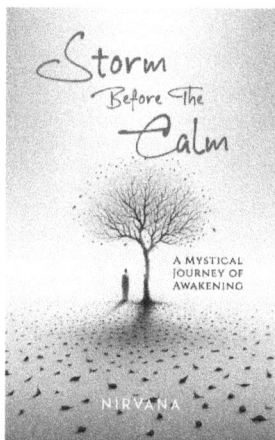

Storm
Before The
Calm

A MYSTICAL
JOURNEY OF
AWAKENING

NIRVANA

ISBN: 978-1-962685-04-7

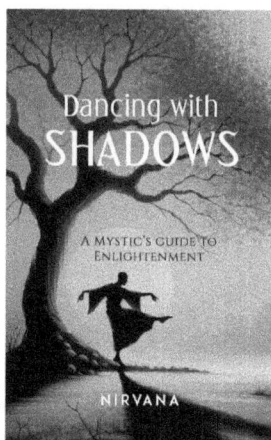

Dancing with
SHADOWS

A MYSTIC'S GUIDE TO
ENLIGHTENMENT

NIRVANA

ISBN: 978-1962685061

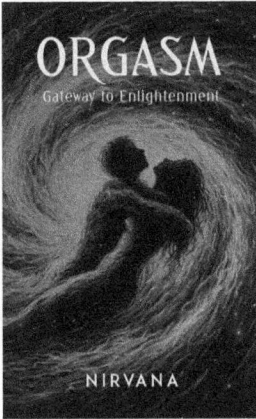

ISBN: 978-1962685085

www.ingramcontent.com/pod-product-compliance
Lightning Source LLC
Chambersburg PA
CBHW031949080426
42735CB00007B/331